On the ROAD to SPIRITUAL WHOLENESS

On the ROAD to SPIRITUAL WHOLENESS

Flora Slosson Wuellner

Abingdon/Nashville

On the Road to Spiritual Wholeness

Copyright © 1978 by Abingdon

All rights reserved.
No part of this book may be reproduced in any manner whatsoever without written permission of the publisher except brief quotations embodied in critical articles or reviews. For information address Abingdon, Nashville, Tennessee.

Library of Congress Cataloging in Publication Data

WUELLNER, FLORA SLOSSON.
  On the road to spiritual wholeness.
  1. Spiritual life. I. Title.
  BV4501.2.W83   248'.48   77-12232

ISBN 0-687-28920-3

Scripture quotations are from the Revised Standard Version Common Bible, copyrighted © 1973.

MANUFACTURED BY THE PARTHENON PRESS AT
NASHVILLE, TENNESSEE, UNITED STATES OF AMERICA

This book is affectionately dedicated to
the Rev. and Mrs. H. L. Pickerill
(lovingly known as "the Picks"
to hundreds of students),
who by their joint ministry guided so many of us,
in our sensitive years,
into the health of the spirit

Foreword

This book, based on many of my own mistakes and growth experiences, was written out of deep concern over a growing menace to our spiritual health in the 1970s.

Seventeen years ago, as a young pastor, I began to explore and to participate in the vast and mysterious energies of prayer. Prayer was then a largely untapped source in the life of the average Christian and the average church, and it became my specialized ministry to work on the spiritual growth front as teacher, prayer leader, counselor, and writer.

But during these recent years, when spiritual enthusiasm has grown incredibly in so many ways and so

ON THE ROAD TO SPIRITUAL WHOLENESS

many places, it has become clear that ardent faith and fervent prayer are not enough to ensure spiritual wholeness. With dismay, I have seen that the energy of prayer itself can become a menace to spiritual health if based on a foundation of compulsiveness. Visiting and leading groups, counseling seekers, searching my own heart, I see how easily the power of prayer can be used to repress, intimidate, control, and compel.

We are on the threshold of a new—and yet very ancient—spiritual danger. But once awakened, we can't go back to slumber and indifference. We can't go back into any kind of protective shell. The only answer is to go onward to the unfaced depths within, where the living Christ reveals, heals, releases.

This book is concerned with God's new, and threatened, creation—the whole human being.

Contents

1. A New Spiritual Danger *13*
2. Our Hidden Wholeness *23*
3. Prayer—a Doorway to Wholeness *37*
4. New Moral Discovery *56*
5. Test Signs of Spiritual Growth *71*
6. The Free Christian and Group Commitment *84*
7. A Suggested Spiritual Retreat or Workshop *98*

On the ROAD to SPIRITUAL WHOLENESS

Chapter 1

A New Spiritual Danger

The prayer of thousands of people is being answered now, in our generation. But whenever God gives an answer, he asks a question!

For so many years, so many of us have been praying for a religious awakening, a spiritual revival. From the large church councils to the smallest prayer group, from the pope to the Ladies Aid, we have prayed for the visitation of the Holy Spirit.

We knew something more was needed in our churches and in our hearts. We began to admit our inner hunger and our failing energy. We knew we were like dry wells. We needed new waters to feed our thirst. We knew we were full of unanswered questions,

ON THE ROAD TO SPIRITUAL WHOLENESS

straining our will power and our good intentions. There must be something more to being a Christian, we thought, than active committees, balanced budgets, theological correctness, good intentions. Surely there was a radiance, a power, an inner strength of love which would not just *talk*, but would change lives. Jesus had promised it. The early churches had it. All through history, new leaders and groups aflame with the Spirit had, in their own transformation, changed the world around them. We prayed for this to happen again.

The answer has been explosive beyond all reckoning. Like wildfire, within a decade new spiritual life movements, charismatic groups, dedicated communities have spread across the country. New, radiant witnesses to the power of the Spirit have risen within and outside the churches. Some are Christian, sharing the Lord on street corners, in groups and communes, singing, talking, praying in new strange ways. Some are of faiths from the Far East, witnessing to different manifestations of God, chanting on the streets, seeking out converts, building new centers.

We saw lives being actually changed—young lives and old lives too. Under the power of prayer we saw addictions broken. We saw genuine healing of bodies and minds. Radiance, direction, purpose came into weak and drifting lives. We saw moral strength and discipline.

But as time went on, we saw something else that

A NEW SPIRITUAL DANGER

began to alarm us. In the midst of the exciting new spiritual fire and change, in the midst of the love and the prayer, we saw the shape of a new problem, a new danger. *For whenever God answers a prayer, he asks a deeper question!* A depth question, a challenge. He waits for us to hear it, to see it, to ask ourselves, and then to grow deeper.

This is the question: Are you able to take the power of religious awakening, and continue to grow in human wholeness?

He has asked this question before. Repeatedly. In times past, along with the great creative good of aroused religious fervor has come also intolerance, witch hunts, unspeakable persecution, religious wars, abuse of the body and its energies, abuse of the psychic powers and gifts, the crushing of the free spirit of humankind. If religious awakening arouses the most beautiful and compassionate energies, it also arouses the most savage and crushing energies—often in the same person or group.

The greater and more divine the power, the greater and more devastating the possible abuse. So that is why whenever God gives such gifts as love, patriotism, control over nature, clairvoyance, political charisma, atomic energy—and above all, religious fervor—he asks the question: Are you ready for this? Can you remain human and whole? And in the agony of our growing and learning we often wish to answer, "No. We are not ready."

ON THE ROAD TO SPIRITUAL WHOLENESS

What is our answer now as we look at the ferment on the religious waterfront? There are definitely some signs to alarm us. We are seeing new methods and procedures in many spiritual growth groups which wipe out human freedom, individual identity, and human wholeness.

Most of us are familiar now with the tactics of the large, notorious "mind-bending" groups. They have been well publicized, these dehumanizing identity-obliterating movements drawing to them the spiritually hungry and drifting. We are learning to be alert and watchful about the more obvious abuses of spiritual power, in its threat to education, the economy, and government. We are apt to ignore the fact that the abuse of any power does not begin with misguided people "out there." It begins in our own hearts. In most of us there is some willingness to use power to twist the lives of others. In most of us there is willingness to let ourselves be used and twisted. The more powerful, gifted, and beautiful the one wielding the power, the greater the temptation to dominate or surrender. *This is spiritual assault, often going on under the name of spiritual growth.*

Not long ago I visited a quiet, respectable group of fifty or seventy people, meeting in a private home as was their custom. Their leader was a woman of magnetism, charm, and eloquence. Fascinated, I sat, listening to her teachings expressed with insight and power. "Why are your hands trembling?" whispered my

A NEW SPIRITUAL DANGER

daughter after we'd been listening for a half hour. Startled, I realized she was right. I realized I was feeling invaded, frightened. I looked around and watched the faces of others. They looked anxious and submissive. The room seemed full of strain and fear. This gifted, commanding woman was guiding them by fear. I noticed how often she would single out a member of the group, speak at length of his or her personal blocks and faults, and rebuke the person before us all. I noticed no one attempted explanation or defense, and certainly not argument. The only response permitted was total submission or request for more punishing analysis. One of the members explained to me later that any thought or act of defense or resistance was a sign of obtrustive "ego," which must be humiliated and crushed if the person wished to grow spiritually and morally.

Many of the members of this group have changed remarkably since they joined. Bad habits have been dropped, and moral power has taken on muscle. They are gentle, scrupulous, honest, and chaste. But they have lost their spontaneity. All that they feel, think, and say is watched and judged. They are trained to watch themselves, to watch one another, and above all to submit to the watchfulness of the leader. No decision is made without her. Anyone who wishes to leave the group is told he or she is headed for spiritual degeneration. Her energy field fills and commands any room in which she speaks. Submission to this energy field is

ON THE ROAD TO SPIRITUAL WHOLENESS

called submission to God. Is this lock-step experience a spiritual growth, or only spiritual obedience? They are not the same.

Very different was the method of spiritual assault used by another magnetic leader many miles away. As I sat in his group, I was aware not of punishment or fear, but of joy and beauty. His way of talking, his presence seemed to heighten one's awareness in every way. He did not humiliate his followers, but praised and delighted in their response. His members clustered around, tape-recording his conversation, their faces shining with enthusiasm and agreement. I noticed how their shoes were also shining. Every man wore a tie and jacket, every girl a long dress.

After an hour and a half I rose to go. "You are resisting me," the leader said calmly. Surprised, I sat down again. "Ah," he said approvingly. "Now your face has lost its defensiveness. I see again that beautiful expression of trust."

The conversation continued, and I noticed how his spiritual advice to me centered increasingly around the necessity for surrender, submission, *now!* To God or to him? I wondered. Or were they one and the same in his thinking? And what about Jesus' counsel to pray to God, surrender to God quietly in one's own room?

The next day I met with two of his followers. They played the taped conversation. No interpretation or argument on my part was permitted. Only one line of thought was to be followed, and nothing new or un-

A NEW SPIRITUAL DANGER

programmed might be introduced. I felt as if I were talking not to two human beings, but to two amplifiers. I was not treated as a human being either, but as an object with a faulty working mechanism which they would set right. Was this spiritual growth going on, or spiritual depersonalization?

By now I have visited many groups where growth and assault are confused. Some are rigidly structured organizations; others are loosely organized. Some make a big point of dress and ritual; others couldn't care less. In some, the leaders rule by fear; in others, by gentleness. Some stamp out rebellious thoughts with exorcism, and others with gentle, persistent reasoning and prayer. Some downgrade women; others make no distinction between the sexes. Some depend on a written book of rules, others on the command of a leader. Some are connected with organized churches, and some are independent. Some have hundreds of members, others three or four.

But one thing they all have in common. *They all have a deep and growing suspicion of free, individual spontaneity and uniqueness.* There are structured patterns for spiritual and moral growth. A programmed response is expected and urged forth. A childlike dependency and submissiveness is considered the groundwork for true spiritual growth. Questioning, doubt, reserve are treated as unhealthy or demonic forces which must be suppressed. In short, spiritual

ON THE ROAD TO SPIRITUAL WHOLENESS

growth is equated with merging into the group identity.

A gentle young woman came to see me once and told me she was leaving such a group because, in spite of the joy, prayer, and close fellowship there, she felt her personal being was increasingly swallowed up. I was not surprised when she showed me the printed statement of the group's purpose, which read: "The basis of loving unity is authority and submission." Her doubts and questions had been interpreted as her ego's rebellion against God. She had been told that if she made a permanent and complete commitment to the group, her problems would be solved and her doubts would melt away.

Why would a vital, intelligent person choose such a superstructure of authority, such a programmed, absolutist approach to spiritual growth? We can see why as we look around at the moral jungle of our present culture and see the confused groping of many of our political, educational and religious leaders. We have seen the extremes of moral permissiveness in ourselves, our churches and families. We have seen the rootlessness, loneliness, lack of moral accountability and maturity. We have seen people—even people with genuine spiritual aspirations—living at the mercy of the inner fragmented self and shifting desires.

"My prayer life seems to be difficult and dim these days," a young woman once said to me. "Am I using some wrong methods?" I knew she was living a life of

A NEW SPIRITUAL DANGER

sexual promiscuity and irresponsibility. She honestly couldn't see a real connection.

A young minister permitted his fifteen-year-old daughter to leave home and drift around the country. "I must let her live her own life, mustn't I?" he asked in genuine bewilderment. "I mustn't be an authoritarian parent."

A young man, well known to me, left wife, children, and job, and under "guidance" wandered around the country having mystical experiences and vague relationships with equally uncommitted partners. He admits no guidelines, no structure, no commitments. He is accountable only to himself. Every time I see him, he looks more "un-jelled."

Having seen, and maybe also having experienced, this kind of vague, chaotic "spiritual" life in which no strong moral muscle seems to develop, many persons turn to the authoritarian groups to give them the firm direction they hunger for. Others, impatient with what they feel is their slow growth in spiritual awareness, or lonely in their spiritual search, are willing to join a strong group in order to advance swiftly. Some, feeling in themselves a strong idealistic energy, get impatient with the main-line churches, and feel in their forums, discussion groups, permissive listening to both sides of every question that they aren't getting anywhere. They are willing to merge their individual identity with a strong group in order to bring about more rapid changes in the world. Some are longing for the strong, supportive companionship of people who are concerned about them, even when that concern is shown through supervision, interference, or even punishment. Some have found a teacher whom they deeply admire and who seems to have genuine spiritual insight. They are willing to commit themselves in obedience so they can share the energy, light, and power of that teacher. Others have experienced a religious or psychic "awakening" at a depth level and, knowing they need guidance, have joined themselves to the first powerful, committed group that they found, not knowing there are alternatives. There are many reasons for abandoning the pain and ambiguity of personal identity in spiritual search.

Most of us will not choose either extreme of the moral jungle or the moral straitjacket. But perhaps we have friends or family members who have chosen one or the other of these extremes. We suffer as we watch them drifting from one spiritual fad to another, or gripped and held fast by a depersonalizing spiritual superstructure. We wonder if there is a real answer. Must the ordinary Christian only muddle through as he seeks spiritual and moral growth? Or must he after all surrender his personal identity and his personal responsibility in order to receive religious power?

Or is there another way?

Chapter 2

Our Hidden Wholeness

Why are we so easily led to assault or submission in our spiritual search? I think it is a deep misunderstanding of what the *self* is. What is the real *I* in each of us? Is it of God or Satan? Is it our only opening to God or our main block? Is it to be glorified or stamped out? Or does it exist at all?

I remember a little verse that was popular among many of us idealistic young people a generation ago: "God first. Others next. Me last." We taped that verse on our mirrors and desk tops to remind us of our priorities as good Christians. We didn't stop to ask what we meant by that "me," that low man on the totem pole. *Why* was it to be last? Was it by nature so much in

ON THE ROAD TO SPIRITUAL WHOLENESS

opposition to God and others that it couldn't be trusted? Was anything we felt we wanted or needed wrong—by definition? Was having a self, being a self, the same as being selfish?

Many spiritually minded people seemed to think so. Many more spiritual groups are growing now that teach so. There are many articles and books that teach us how to "slay the ego." This is a method by which we ask God to humiliate and destroy the assertive, obstructive part of the self. Many people report experiences of trauma and pain as God (or what they call God) does his work on their stubborn selfishness.

Some groups go much further. When they speak of ego-slaying they mean not only the selfishness, but the very personal self. They teach that there is no real "I" at all. Only God exists. Our illusion that we have any kind of a real personal identity is an illusion arising from fear and possessiveness. They teach methods by which a person can wipe out such illusions.

But since most people cannot yet make the final step of true oneness with God, the next best thing to settle for is oneness with the group identity. This will, at least, have the practical result of destroying that stubborn ego.

There are many methods by which the self is put down and a suitable receptiveness and pliancy substituted. There may be public rebuke, which members of some groups are taught to use on one another.

"Why do you act so self-conscious?" roared a group

leader to a shy young man in the midst of a group game.

"Stinking ego. That's all it is," said one young woman contemptuously to another woman as she wept at a public scolding.

"I always punish my six-year-old daughter when she gets angry," said one young father to me quite seriously. "She must be taught that anger is not her *real* self."

"Oh, you mustn't feel that way," said a prayer leader to a member who had expressed a worry. "Christians don't feel afraid, you know."

"Well, you've just probably paid for some sins," said one member calmly to another, who had just accidentally burned herself.

The individual is reminded persistently in every situation that his or her personal wishes, choices, reactions, and opinions are unimportant. He is taught he will outgrow them. He is taught to feel guilty about strong feelings and to repress them instantly. The individual is treated as the "blob" of science fiction treats its human victim. It inexorably rolls over the victim, surrounds, and digests him, so that it may become "one" with him.

We can tell when a person's "self" has been digested. He is determinedly cheerful, friendly, relentlessly positive, but there is no more spontaneous reaction from his own unique thoughts. He speaks only what the group speaks through him. He observes only what the group observes. He does not ask a real question, nor is

ON THE ROAD TO SPIRITUAL WHOLENESS

he interested in any answer from an outsider; because not only is he no longer aware of his own identity, he is also unaware that you, the listener, are a real separate "self" with something to offer. You are an object out there which exists only to be drawn into oneness with him.

At the opposite extreme from digestion of the self is glorification of some one *part* of the self. This approach does not try to stamp out the ego—far from it. But it does something almost as dangerous. It concentrates on only one aspect of the person's self and feelings, and treats that aspect like God.

A man once came to talk with me about an emotional problem. He had been meek and submissive all his life. Encouraged by an encounter group to express his anger whenever he felt it, it took over his life. He became no longer a man who feels anger; he has become an angry man.

A woman in a similar group became aware of her neglected need to be cherished and protected. She allowed herself to make that one need the pivotal point of her relationships. Now all she can do is cling, be carried and dominated.

Another man realized he had been sexually afraid and repressed all his life. Encouraged to listen primarily to that need only, he gave himself free rein. Now his sexuality controls him, making his decisions for him, crowding out other needs and experiences.

These three persons, and many like them, have

taken one part of the self and magnified it into the *whole*. They seldom ask themselves, "Is this feeling, this need, the main part of me or only a fragment of me? If I allow it energy without limit, will it take over other parts of me? Am I ignoring other, perhaps deeper, needs by listening only to this one?"

It is dangerously easy to swing from the exaltation of the fragmentary self to stern repression of the total self. Both are based on a serious misunderstanding of what this self is that God has given us.

What is a healthy answer for the Christian as, with the Spirit of Christ, he asks the age-old question: Who am I?

The fragments and surfaces answer first. And they must be heard, listened to, for they are part of us. "I am a woman," "I am a business man." "I am a black person," "I am old." This is the outer, physically embodied person answering.

"Who am I?" we ask our emotions. The answers surge back: "I am an impulsive person." "I am restless." "I am lonely." "I enjoy things." "I'm in pain" or "I need other people" or "I'm shy and like to be alone." These are important parts of ourselves, these feelings. They are to be heard.

"Who am I?" we ask our purposeful self—our will, our plans, our ideals. And we hear responses: "I want to make my life count in some way." "I want to make life better for my children." "I want to feel I can do things and change things—maybe in politics or in business." "I

ON THE ROAD TO SPIRITUAL WHOLENESS

want to understand some of the mysteries of the universe." "I want to create something—art, writing, inventions." "I want to make my home a happy, beautiful one for my family."

"Who am I?" we ask our memories. We are surprised to see what floats up in memories of pain and joy, humiliation and triumph. Sometimes they are such small, insignificant things we wonder why they are memories at all. What are they telling us about ourselves? Are we still that shy little girl, that curious little boy inside? Are we still that unsure, but eager, adolescent inside? Do we still have that feeling of being a failure or a disappointment to others that we had that time twenty years ago? Are we really a person so deeply aware of the world's beauty still? That memory seems to say we are.

"Who am I?" we ask as we look into the lightless depths of the subconscious. We don't know what is there. We suspect some things through our dreams, especially the ones that keep coming back. We guess some things through habit patterns that seem so strong, or the kinds of events or persons that seem to come so often into our lives. What is going on down there? We know the subconscious self has its own answer to give.

"Who am I?" we ask what we call the "superconscious" self, or the soul. Perhaps its answer comes promptly, either from our religious doctrine or through experiences and thoughts long ago worked over and

OUR HIDDEN WHOLENESS

expressed. Perhaps the answer comes slowly and hesitantly as we try to think, maybe for the first time, what certain experiences of joy, exultation, ecstasy, mystery might mean. We grope for an answer as we know *some*thing in us is telling us that we share somehow in eternal purposes. That we matter somehow to Eternal Love. It is hard sometimes to hear the answer from this deep part of the self, but we know that it is there and that it has spoken. And that it speaks.

Which of these answers comes from the "true" self? We look at the Christ of the Gospels, we see how he spoke to people, responded to them on all levels from their crudest physical needs to their subtlest mystical insights. There was no level of the human being that he ignored. "You are the light of the world," he said to one group, seeing their growing, eager energies. He saw other crowds and spoke of them as distraught and helpless, like sheep without a shepherd. He saw and fed their physical hunger. He fed the spiritual hunger of Nicodemus. He talked with promiscuous women on a level they understood, and to money hungry tax-collectors on a level they understood. He spoke to mothers about their children and to priests about their sermons and to farmers about their harvests and to fishermen about their nets.

He met each person where that person was *at*, and fed his or her need at its deepest level. Each fragmentary part of the person was faced and accepted fully with recognition, humor, compassion, firmness. "You

ON THE ROAD TO SPIRITUAL WHOLENESS

are legion," he said to one sick man, meaning, "There are many selves inside you, many fragments, many pieces, many energies." But underlying the physical, emotional, intellectual, purposeful parts, *he saw the whole person.* He saw the enduring, mysterious beauty and uniqueness which we can't see yet. He saw the divine pattern of wholeness which holds the parts, the fragments, the levels in its embrace.

And through all his parables, metaphors, dialogues, he tells us over and over that each of us is an eternal, unique, precious being which God cherishes and seeks as the shepherd seeks the lamb, or the parent the lost child. As we see ourselves through Jesus' eyes, we see someone unutterably dear and beautiful, as the bride is to the bridegroom. We see a self filled with creative divine energy, as a pregnant mother is filled with child, or a loaf of bread is filled with the mystery of the yeast.

And this deep self is not just a potential being—not just someone who will someday exist if we try hard enough. It exists now. There is an old legend that each person has a secret hidden face which only God sees. Spiritual growth takes place when that face, unlike any other face in all creation, is allowed to shine through.

When Christ looked at a person, he saw not only the sick, restless, weeping parts, but also that secret, unique face. And he spoke with fellowship and challenge to that deep self as a spiritual brother or sister.

In his spirit, we learn the same relationship to a person's wholeness. We learn to look with compassionate awareness at the outer and visible man, woman, and child. We learn to tune in lovingly to their emotional needs. We also learn to salute that secret, eternal self which is so seldom able to shine through.

"But isn't that just the problem?" say the spiritually authoritarian. "Those outer selves, the body, the restless emotions, the negative thoughts, those possessive needs—aren't these the very things that *hide* that deep self? Shouldn't we push aside and destroy those obstructions? If they are not the deep self, but just fragments of the self, why relate to them at all?"

But Jesus Christ did relate to those more surface, fragmented selves. He related to them as we would relate to a restless child. He does not destroy these fragments. He heals and fulfills. He shows us that each fragment, broken though it is, is a hint at the beauty of the whole.

A poignant example of this is his dealing with the Samaritan woman drawing water from the well, in the fourth chapter of John's Gospel. Each aspect of herself as both a human and an eternal being was encountered: her act of drawing water; her physical need for water, and his also; her rootless emotional life; and finally her deeper need, which thirsted for "living water."

In every relationship we are shown in the Gospels, Jesus treated the physical and emotional self with dignity and concern. And if he sensed the time was ripe, he challenged the deeper self, the hidden wholeness.

Why does the Christ deal so gently with our surface

ON THE ROAD TO SPIRITUAL WHOLENESS

selves, our fragmented selves? Why doesn't he destroy the obstructions? Why is his spirit of growth never that of assault? Because these fragmented parts of ourselves are not just tumors to be cut out. They are *energies,* parts of our whole selves, once part of God's energy—and therefore once beautiful. *He baptizes our energies, and heals them. He does not kill them.* He restores them, whatever they are, to their original beauty.

Try an experiment. Look at some fault or block of yours which troubles you. Ask yourself, What was this twisted energy when it was beautiful?

Take anger, for example. It is a strong energy. Like all energy, it originally came from God and was once beautiful. What was it, this power, originally? What was the face of anger when it was beautiful? Surely it was the power and passion of justice. If you are an angry person, it means that you are a person born with a strong sense of justice and righteousness. This power has become twisted and distorted, yes, But when God heals it, it will still be a strong power. When this anger is returned to his radiant light for healing, it will become again the beautiful thing it was meant to be. He will not kill your power, your energy. He transforms it and restores it. You will remain a "lion"; he won't turn you into a "lamb."

What about fear and worry? What was that when it was beautiful? The energy that we have turned into fear comes from a power of sensitive awareness. This is

OUR HIDDEN WHOLENESS

a beautiful angel, indeed. It is the very foundation for openness and sensitivity to others. Out of this sensitivity springs the power of art and imagination. When God takes fear into his hands, he will not destroy the underlying sensitivity. He will restore it.

How about sloth and laziness? I have noticed how often sloth afflicts persons of deep, firm integrity, strength, and honor. They are people who won't be rushed, pushed, or dominated. When they get in situations that they do not accept, their answer is to put on the inner brakes, drag the anchor. When God heals the twisted manner of response, he won't destroy the deep integrity, but will release it to express itself in a more creative way.

Sensuality? Surely this arises from a deep awareness of the beauty and power of the sensory world around us, and an ability to participate joyously in the world. Healed sensuality will turn one not into a bodiless hermit, but into a person filled with true joy in life, who looks on physical powers as St. Francis did, brothers and sisters to be companions, not gods to be obeyed.

Perfectionism? Bossiness? Perhaps this is the twisting of the deep need to create, to make one's life count.

Go down the list. Think of all the things in you or others that block, thwart, hurt. Everyone of them, no matter how twisted and perverted, had its original roots in some divine energy, once beautiful.

I am not saying there is no evil. Of course there is evil. Jesus fully faced that fact and took it seriously. I am saying that evil has no *separate* source of power or energy. All energy comes from one source—God. Evil is the twisting and perverting of divine energy. It is the misuse of that free will, which is probably God's divinest gift to us.

How did such a misuse arise? Why the choice to act in a fragmented, destructive way rather than in a wholistic way? There is an old Hebrew legend that Adam was a galactic being, light years tall, with unimaginable energies and gifts flowing to him and through him. Was this the way God had originally envisioned his children, humankind? In whatever form our first consciousness took place, did we rush our attempt to grow and learn, trying to "go faster than grace"? Is that what is symbolized by the story of forbidden fruit? Was it a kind of spiritual "assault" that humankind made on itself, much like the modern taking of psychedelic drugs to force a premature mystical awareness? And when we broke too swiftly into awareness of the potentialities of good and evil, did we feel frightened, insecure? Is that the meaning behind the symbols of Adam's and Eve's instantly clothing themselves? Was it a pathetic desire to defend themselves, and give themselves some kind of shelter?

Does all our fragmentation, and even all our evil, arise from a deep fear and defensiveness? We find it easier to hide than to face and live with ourselves.

Whatever the reason, our conscious decision to act only from a part, a fragment, of ourselves, rather than from the whole of ourselves, has taken the very springs of light and energy within us and twisted that energy into a hurtful power. And the greater the original gift and energy, the worse is its perversion. "If then the light in you is darkness," said Jesus, "how great is the darkness!"

Yet still that spring of light, that fountain of energy, flows continually from God's hands. We can return to those hands the sick, twisted remnants of his energy for healing.

We need not be afraid of those hands. So many of us are. "You know, dear, we are in God's hands," said one woman resignedly in a storm at sea. "Good heavens! I hope we're not as bad off as *that*," replied her frightened companion.

Often in little discussion groups, we admit to one another that we are afraid of putting ourselves in God's hands entirely. We are afraid he will hurt us, humiliate us, or "kill the ego" in some traumatic way—all for our own good. Maybe he'll take away the people or things we love. Maybe he'll so completely change us that we won't be really ourselves any more.

We can face this very human fear, and then we can look at Jesus. And we see those hands came not to destroy but to fulfill. The God he channels to us does not assault us. Certain types of groups may do so. We may do so to ourselves. But the God we see through Jesus does not treat the self or any part of the self in that way. He heals the sick parts. He restores the fragmented

ON THE ROAD TO SPIRITUAL WHOLENESS

parts. He brings us into wholeness, the physical cells, the emotional needs, the hurtful, haunting memories, the cramped powers. *He releases the hidden wholeness of each self, as a unique creation.* In the everlasting feast of joy he has prepared, each voice will be of unique beauty, singing its unique song, as part of that divine harmony. God wills it! We need not fear those hands.

Thus our growing is not a static, patterned response outlined by a rigid authority. Rather it is an organic, vital, open-ended experience, growing out of unfolding mystery. "He shall be like a tree, planted by the water," says the First Psalm, describing the growth of the whole and holy human being. How can we cooperate with that releasing spirit of Christ working in us?

Chapter 3

Prayer—a Doorway to Wholeness

Prayer is the key by which God opens in us the locked doors of our tight inner compartments. Prayer is the means by which he breaks down the walls dividing us within. Prayer is the transfusion of his supreme consciousness directly into our fragmented consciousness. Prayer is the divine yeast working within to change our substance, flesh and spirit, into health and fullness. Through prayer we become his channels, through which he radiates healing and light into a groaning, diseased, and fragmented world. As prayer changes us, we become like radium implants on the cancerous body of the world.

The world is always a little different after we have prayed!

ON THE ROAD TO SPIRITUAL WHOLENESS

It is not just any kind of prayer which changes us and the world around us. Prayer which is dishonest, which plays games with God and the self is perhaps worse than useless. Prayer which is used as an escape from our true feelings and our true condition only serves as another trap. Prayer based on the belief that God is some kind of giant computer, or a whimsical king who must be flattered and begged, or a stern parent whose love must be earned, is a prayer whose foundations are rotten from the start.

I am angered by liturgies which chant wailingly: "We beseech thee to hear us, good Lord," as if the deafness and unwillingness were on the part of God! Such prayers build a doubt and distrust of God's love, right from the beginning. I am saddened by prayers which add a cautious "If it be thy will" after an intercession for healing, as if it could possibly be God's will that a man, woman, or child should die of cancer or in an auto accident. Much that happens in this world is against God's will, including tragic accidents and agonizing illness. Jesus never refused healing to anyone. Sometimes he *couldn't* heal them because of certain conditions which blocked his work, but his desire was always to heal, and he taught clearly that this was also his Father's desire and will. (Anyone still confused on this basic point should read the magnificent little book *The Will Of God*, by Leslie Weatherhead [Nashville: Abingdon Festival Book, 1976].)

If we are in real doubt about how God feels toward

PRAYER—A DOORWAY TO WHOLENESS

us, and what are his intentions toward us, let us turn again to the Twenty-third Psalm and read it every day, night, and morning for several weeks. Read it as if you had never read it before. Perhaps read it using a new translation. This is the supreme song to the God who nurtures us and does not assault us.

Or read again the timeless story of the wasteful son (Luke 15:11-32) returning to his home after many useless years. Read it as if it were the first time you had ever heard such an interpretation of God's nature. Let it sink deep into the subconscious, healing the roots of fear. Think of him as one who waits and watches for our slightest sign of turning around. Think of him as one who *runs* swiftly to meet us at our first sign of response. Think of him as one who welcomes us just as we are, no matter what a negative mess we may have become. Think of him as one who rejoices in us, and shares all abundance with us, even as we are challenged to take up the work of child and partner.

> With thee is the fountain of life.
>
> They feast on the abundance of thy house.
>
> He restores my soul.
>
> In thy presence there is fullness of joy.

With this growing assurance of the nurturing, challenging Consciousness around us, and a radiant, healing energy streaming into us, we can enter with confi-

ON THE ROAD TO SPIRITUAL WHOLENESS

dence into healthy prayer, which is the ultimate way of saying yes to God on all the levels of body, feelings, mind, spirit.

A good, practical way to begin is to put the physical body under the energy and light of the Christ. Some picture a cloak of white or golden light covering the whole body from the head to the feet. As you quietly breathe, think how every breath is drawing in divine energy and strength. Think of his healing waters pouring into every part of the body, every cell and organ. If any parts of the body are in special pain, tension, or strain, send the waters of light especially to those parts. Let the stiff mask of the face melt, so the true face can shine through. Picture the top of the head opening like a window, so more divine light can stream in. Encourage the body to become a relaxed and shining channel of the work of the spirit.

Turn the attention now to the surging, restless feelings and emotions. Many people, in prayer, make the mistake of trying to wipe the mind clean of what they consider distracting thoughts and feelings in order to pray for others and listen to God. But that is to assault the self. If we want to cooperate with God's will to make us whole, we must face those inner "children" of fears, angers, irritations, worries, loneliness, self-pity, needs, joys, loves, ambitions. As explained in the last chapter, God understands and confronts us on *all* levels of the self.

Turn the attention to the inner children, the feelings.

PRAYER—A DOORWAY TO WHOLENESS

Ask yourself, "What am I actually feeling now? What have been my strong feelings today?" It is all right to have feelings. Feelings in *themselves* are not sins. Sin only enters the picture when we deliberately promote and sustain negative feelings, refusing to allow them to be healed. Negative feelings will not block God's work through us, *if* we are honest about them and lift them one by one into God's healing light, just as we lift a hurt child and put him into the hands of the doctor.

What about our very human needs and wants? Many people trying to grow spiritually are embarrassed about "bothering" God with their personal needs. They feel they are being selfish about expressing their needs when there are so many people in the world in greater need. Or perhaps they have been taught that spiritual growth means that we will become detached from human needs, floating, so to speak, above ordinary human cravings. This is a false and dangerous teaching. It assaults our human wholeness in incarnational life. It is not borne out by the teaching and life of Jesus who taught us to pray for our daily bread, who respected human physical and emotional needs in others, who never scorned the body, who was always thankful for fellowship, rest, food; who wept when sad, who dreaded pain, who needed a strong companion to help carry the cross.

Undoubtedly, as we grow we will *out*grow many things that at our present level we consider to be needs. Certain habits, hang-ups, and obsessions that we know to be limiting to our wholeness will someday be outgrown. We will become free of many things that we feel completely dependent on now. But basic needs we will always have, and the spiritually whole person will rejoice in that fact of humanity.

Take the simple fact of being hungry and eating. Spiritual growth usually means a change on two fronts here. As we become more spiritually aware, we become *more* delightedly aware of the goodness of food, and thankful when we have it. At the same time we healthily outgrow obsessions about overeating, or undereating and fussy hang-ups about exactly what we eat. We enjoy it more, but are less dependent.

Or take the need for human love and close companionship. As we grow spiritually we become more aware of the need to be warmly close to others, as well as of the preciousness and uniqueness of those around us. But also we begin to outgrow possessiveness and overdependency.

In short, we grow into awareness of what are our deep, true needs as human beings, and what are the sick, limiting needs that can be outgrown. But the only way to grow is to face with honesty *all* our needs—the healthy, the unhealthy, and those we are not so sure about—and hold them all in Christ's healing light.

What about our problems and plans? We can begin by facing our problem as clearly as we can, taking into account all the facts of the situation that we know. Then put the whole bundle into the hands of Christ. In the next few days, watch expectantly for a vital solution to take shape in your thoughts, or a change in the facts and realities around you. This does not mean that we become helpless little children pushed around by God, incapable of vigorous thought and decision. Many strong people are put off religion by this false image, and unfortunately many spiritual growth cults actually seem to promote the image of the spiritual person as a kind of jellyfish or floating seaweed or immature child.

On the contrary, our strength grows, our independence grows, our ability to make decisions and take responsibility grows. But by placing our problems and plans in the light of Christ (which is around us when we pray) we are enabled to contact, tune in on, deeper levels of the self, a wider vision of the situation than is possible otherwise. *God's act on us is always to make us more whole, not more childishly dependent!* It is not childish dependence to be made more aware of deeper realities than are usually available to normal consciousness.

Let's turn to memories as we pray. More than we realize we are haunted by old, unreleased, unhealed memories. Many of them are as alive to us now as when we first had the experience. Maybe more so. Try an experiment: think back to the earliest fear, the earliest humiliation, or the earliest anger you can recall. Isn't it still very alive and painful?

Once when I was leading a prayer for the healing of memories at a retreat, one elderly lady came up to me afterward with tears in her eyes. "It all came back to me just now," she whispered. "I was about five or six. I was entering a new Sunday school, and I had on my new pink dress. A girl came up and asked me if that was my Sunday dress, and when I said yes so happily, she said 'Well, it isn't pretty.' I thought I'd forgotten all that long ago. But it still hurts."

Why should an apparently trivial memory linger so long with such pain? There *are* no trivial memories. Whatever remains in memory remains there because it symbolizes something for us. One incident may actually incarnate a deep, underlying fear, a long-term discomfort or tension, or profound purpose. Or an incident may be the traumatic moment of breakthrough to a new realization either joyful or painful. When a memory comes, it is trying to tell us something about ourselves.

Sometimes the memory will be not of one incident but of a long drawn-out time of pain. One of my dear friends, an elderly woman, a beloved prayer and community leader, in the last weeks of her life shared with us the experience of years of pain as a little child. In the early part of the century, her family moved to a rural area. They were of a different church than their neighbors in that farming community, and their religion was not understood or accepted. Unknown to her parents, even apparently unknown to her teacher, the little girl was completely ostracized by the other children at school. They had been ordered by their parents not to play with her or even to speak to her unless absolutely necessary. "Each day at recess," she told us, "I would sit on the back steps of the little school with my head hidden in my lap. The others never came near me. They never looked at me—never in six years." We asked her if she had ever told her parents or her teacher or her church leaders (their church was many miles away, and they could only go once a month). "No," she said. "I never told anyone. And I never cried."

Years and years in childhood, being ignored by those with whom one had to live and work every day, was never shared, never wept over, never healed until old age. That small girl was still in her, alive, in pain, but covered over by decades of activity and service. This is true of many of the most active, cheerful, and serviceable among us. In so many people, often in the ones we would suspect last, the crying child is still there. But God's love makes no account of years or buried layers. It can go directly to the hurt or lonely child within each of us, and comfort and heal it. But we must first become aware of the need.

Old unreleased, unhealed angers and resentments can also be reached and healed. One Easter weekend I was in bed with such a bad cold that I couldn't even read. I lay in the darkness, with my mind vaguely wandering through many disconnected thoughts. Suddenly I became aware that I was clenching teeth and hands with anger over something that had happened two years before. It was an incident I thought I had reasoned through, forgiven and forgotten. And here it

ON THE ROAD TO SPIRITUAL WHOLENESS

was, alive as ever, totally unforgiven, and certainly not forgotten! I was as mad as if it had happened that very morning!

"What else haven't I forgiven?" I wondered. I began to think back to my earliest memories of things that had made me angry. I realized with shock that most of them were still alive and burning in me. I stopped at everyone I could think of and pulled each of them out, like a burning coal from a mattress. I laid them before God.

"These things have been smoldering away for years, deep in my thoughts. I know this is not healthy either for the tissues of my body or for the levels of my consciousness. But apparently I can't heal and forget these things through mere will power and determination. God, please take each one of these smoldering old angers and wash it in your waters of healing." And one by one, I dropped them into the ocean of God's light.

My next step was to think over, as honestly as I could, all the things I had done to make others angry or afraid. This was not a "guilt trip." Many of these things were unintentional. Many were perhaps necessary. But that was not the point. The point was that, justified or not, I had often put these burning coals in other people's mattresses, and there they probably were, smoldering away and doing harm. Perhaps the other person had also thought he or she had forgiven and forgotten. Maybe the other person had grown enough spiritually to release the hurt or anger and be healed. But in any case, I prayed for them, offering myself up as a channel so that Christ's healing waters would inundate the negative energy I had set loose in those persons' lives.

All this was done slowly, clearly, and deliberately. It took a long time, and was both joyful and very painful. At the end, I felt I had been hard at work, creative work. I went to sleep and dreamed of swimming and diving into pools of marvelous coolness and freshness.

I did not wake up as a completely regenerated woman bursting with love and forgiveness. I'm the slow type. Change takes a long time with me. But I did wake up with an improved cold and a much lighter heart. As the weeks and months went on, I noticed that those former memories, though not completely healed or gone, had lost most of their power to hurt or depress. Understanding and compassion began to grow, and even amusement. Things took on a more normal proportion. The memories, though still there, had become increasingly less important, like an outgrown illness.

Do not punish yourself or let others punish you because of old, burning, unhealed memories. Do not let anyone make you feel guilty or unworthy of God's love because you are being honest about old pain and anger and fear. God allows them to surface into our awareness for a good reason—so that we may look at them with compassion, and release them to his love. Most of us do not grow past these things very swiftly. For most of us it takes a long time for the inner wounds to be healed. The timing does not matter. What matters is

ON THE ROAD TO SPIRITUAL WHOLENESS

the general direction our spirit is going and growing. Is it opening toward wholeness, or is it narrowing in on itself and closing off areas of awareness?

What about memories that we can no longer bring to our conscious mind? There were incidents that happened to us long before we were consciously aware or able to express what we felt. Or perhaps there were things so painful or frightening or bewildering that they sank, by necessity, into the depths of our subconscious.

I am deeply interested in a new frontier of prayer these days which deals with prayer for the subconscious. We are taught to release into the hands of the Christ the experience of being carried in the womb, maybe by a mother who did not want us or was afraid or was physically or emotionally ill. Though we cannot consciously remember it, if we suspect there was a problem with our parents at that time, it undoubtedly was affecting us, and we can pray for the unborn child we were, whose feelings of being unwanted are still with us. We can release into Christ's hands the trauma of being born. There is a general raising of consciousness among doctors and psychologists about the shock and pain the newborn child may be experiencing as it emerges from the warm, quiet, close, water-filled life into the chill air, glaring lights, loud noises, having to learn within seconds how to breathe as the lungs expand for the first time in the instantaneous change from a water to an air environment. The shock of being born is probably far worse than the transition of dying. (Surely among churches and prayer groups there should be attention given to this as well as the increasing and wise attention given to the feelings of the dying.)

We can ask Christ's healing touch to reach out to that shock which may still dwell within us, especially if we suspect that our birth experience was unusually prolonged, or if the mother was in great pain or danger, or if instruments had to be used, or if there was difficulty in getting our breathing established.

We can ask his love to flood the deep, buried memories of our earliest days of life when perhaps we were not cuddled enough. Many of those who are now in late middle age were born at a time when mothers were advised to keep their hands off their babies as much as possible, to feed them only on schedule, to allow them to cry for long periods. This emotional and physical starvation undoubtedly is still affecting and hurting many persons who have no memory of all this. It does not matter that we cannot remember. It only matters that we are now willing for Christ's love to flow to those earliest, deepest levels of need and fulfill them *now*.

Perhaps some of us were given up in adoption. It is my opinion that this is a deep and lasting wound, no matter how loving and nurturing the adoptive parents, which needs healing.

Perhaps some of us had parents who in spite of good intentions were blocked in their expression of love. The

ON THE ROAD TO SPIRITUAL WHOLENESS

pain of this can be lifelong, and can severely limit our own expression of love for others. But this too can be healed if we are willing for God's love to flow to the very source.

Perhaps we were separated from our parents at a sensitive age. A middle-aged man once told me that his parents had to leave him for a year when he was three or four, and put him in the care of close friends. He cannot remember any feelings of pain or separation at all, but recently he has begun to wonder if deep buried pain and bewilderment might account for a certain coldness and detachment toward other people which he has always felt.

Perhaps we were hospitalized at a very early age at a time when hospitals did not encourage prolonged visits from parents. Or perhaps a parent was hospitalized or died and we were not told the truth or allowed to share the experience. We were too young to understand all this, and could only defend ourselves by emotional withdrawal.

There is no past in God's eyes or love. All this is present to him now, even as it is alive in us now. And it can be healed at its roots now if we place the bewildered child we were (and are) in his hands.

Perhaps the painful incident happened quite recently, but the shock of it was so great that we did not dare face the full feeling of it. We reasoned it out on the surface, but the deep emotional impact remained untouched. Such a situation was brought to my attention just recently when I talked with an experienced and wise woman healer about a friend who had been in an auto accident a year earlier and was still plagued by much physical pain and emotional tension. "She has prayed, we have prayed, and still there is little improvement," I told her. "She has great faith and is spiritually deeply developed. What is wrong?" The woman healer thought in silence for a few minutes and then said: "Yes, you have prayed about her present pain, but have you prayed about the moment of the accident? I sense that the shock of that moment is still unfaced, unhealed."

I felt this was very likely. My friend had told me that directly after the accident (which was not fatal to anyone, but had given them all a bad shaking) she had been mainly concerned with the driver of the other car who was bleeding slightly and having hysterics. She did not take the time, then or later, to think about or pray for her own feelings of shock and fear. I shared this insight with her, and she prayed for herself as undergoing the trauma of that moment. She has noted a marked improvement.

Very often our feelings of fear, anger, grief, and shock are buried under the crisis of the time by the necessity for action. Crisis and emergencies are a sort of anesthetic to our feelings. Anyone who has faced an emergency illness in the family, or lost a loved one through unexpected death, knows this to be true. There is often a sense of dreamlike detachment that

ON THE ROAD TO SPIRITUAL WHOLENESS

may last a long time. This is a great mercy which enables us to endure what must be endured and to accomplish what must be done. But the feelings are there—most certainly there. And sooner or later we must face the grief, the shock, the pain, or it will torment us in countless undercover ways. It is spiritual assault to tell a person, "You shouldn't be thinking about or dwelling on the past. As a Christian, you should be living only in the present, and having by now only positive feelings of joy, comfort, courage." Refuse this false guilt. Go with God boldly to the moment that you suspect is causing trouble, even though you cannot *consciously* remember anything about it, or even consciously *feel* anything about it. Ask him to take that moment, which is far deeper than you can feel anymore, into his hands and do with it whatever needs to be done.

Sometimes the deepest unfaced fear in the subconscious is that mentioned in the previous chapter—the fear of God himself, fear of the very one of whom we are calling for healing, the very one whose love we know we need. One of my daughters, when a small child, would ask me to sit at the foot of her bed and talk with her for awhile after the lights were out. Somtimes a companionable silence would fall, and then suddenly out of the darkness would come a frightened little voice: "Are you *sure* you're not a gorilla?" All she could see in the dark was the outline of my head and shoulders against the light of the doorway beyond. A lively and sensitive imagination did the rest! After reassuring her, I thought this over. In the midst of the amusement and compassion, I could feel how deeply human this was. How often in the midst of deep and loving prayer, a frightened thought would creep in: "How do I *know* that God is really there? How do I *know* he really loves me? Perhaps it is really only darkness out there, or only an unfeeling, unaware Force of life, someone who doesn't know or care about our pain and our need." Most of us, at one time or another, have looked through the darkness for the face of the Father and asked him, "Are you *sure* you're not a gorilla? " (Apologies, by the way, to gorillas, who, an expert tells me, are actually very sensitive and loving mammals, especially to their young!)

If we who have experienced loving parents have these occasional frightened doubts, how much more the doubt and fear of those whose parents, or other close adults, abused their trust and poisoned for them the very sources of their trust in a loving Creator. If you suspect that the very fountain of life's energy has been poisoned for you that way, go with honesty to the tainted Source, and tell God that deep down you are probably afraid of him and resentful of him, and ask him to heal that fear beneath all fear.

This will not come as news or a shock to God. He has always known what we felt, but nevertheless, with every moment we live and with every breath we draw, he offers again his all-accepting, all-transforming love.

ON THE ROAD TO SPIRITUAL WHOLENESS

In our prayer group, we always have a special time of silence in which we ask Christ to come with his light into the deepest chambers of the subconscious and heal whatever needs healing there. In my own personal prayer at that point, I picture a trapdoor in the floor. When it opens, I remain at the top while the Christ descends the ladder into the dark, unknown depths with his lantern in his hands. I can't see what he is doing, but I know he is moving around in that darkness, opening old trunks, cleaning out dirt and cobwebs, putting together broken pieces. Also, I know he is finding frightened children hiding down there, buried so deeply that I didn't even hear their cries anymore. Is he finding monsters and devils down there? (Many of us are afraid of what long-buried energies may surface.) He may indeed find creatures of distorted shape, pathetic or even menacing. But these, too, were once children of beauty and meaning, and can be healed in his light—every one of them.

Once when I talked of the subconscious in this way to a group, a woman came up afterward and said: "You talk as if the subconscious were nothing but a dirty old basement. You forget that there also are levels of the subconscious deeply in touch with God and the ultimate light. You forget that our newborn energies lie there, still in their beauty, ready for flowering. You forget that there are all the lovingly laid away memories of everything good, precious, and beautiful that has ever happened to us."

PRAYER—A DOORWAY TO WHOLENESS

She was right, and I admitted it. It is not only healing that Christ is doing there in that realm unknown to our surface selves. He is bringing to birth, he is releasing, he is fulfilling. When we pray for the subconscious, even as the past is healed, his divine energy is bringing forth new powers, new gifts in us.

There will be many changes within the weeks and months after we begin faithfully praying for the subconscious self. Some forgotten memories will surface for deliberate facing and releasing. Dreams will begin to change in symbolism and significance. New emotions will emerge, some of pain and some of joy. We will gradually find it easier to laugh, weep, share, touch.

The prayer through Christ for the subconscious is a prayer of immeasurable power. Incredible change begins. One of the greatest changes is the new moral awareness and new moral shape that grows within us as we become more whole.

Chapter 4
New Moral Discovery

"Come to life!" is God's basic challenge to every particle of the universe. It is the deep call to each one of us. We are to wake up, become aware. We are to stretch, look around, grow, ask questions, make mistakes, learn, laugh, weep, touch, discover, commit, create, be surprised—and then grow some more. He wants us to get in touch with and release to light all that we are. He wants us to experience all the beautiful, unique powers sleeping within.

This is what begins to happen through prayer, as we are healed, made whole, and learn to listen. When God begins to wake us up, he moves with gentle, but inexorable, power through one level of ourselves after

NEW MORAL DISCOVERY

another. He never gives us more than we can bear to face or to handle. As we are healed and pulled together into wholeness, we are shown many things that we had not seen before. We are shown feelings we have had, but which have been repressed. We are shown things we have done, judgments we have made during our days of blindness and insensitivity. We are shown relationships in a new light, and facts to which we had not awakened. And as we wake and see, *decisions* about what we see begin to rise in freshness and power.

It is not so much that we are given answers in prayer. We grow into answers!

Our moral awareness, which forms our decisions about right and wrong, arises in this way. As our spiritual consciousness is raised, our moral awareness always changes. It becomes no longer an absolutist set of rules handed to us by some group or leader or even our own sense of duty. Rather, it becomes what it was always meant to be: the deep, direct communication between God's supreme Spirit and our own spirits, which are part of him—and from that profound level our surface, conscious self is awakened.

Our new moral discovery may come swiftly, or it may take a long time to grow, depending on how many blocks are in the way. But when it comes, it will grow organically, asymmetrically, flexibly, individually.

Let us beware of mechanical morals and plastic, assembly-line responses. Remember the example in the First Psalm of the righteous person's being like a

ON THE ROAD TO SPIRITUAL WHOLENESS

tree planted by water. No two trees are ever exactly alike, even those which bear the same name and the same fruit. In my garden at home, when I was a child, there were many apple trees. It was endlessly fascinating to me to wander from one to the other, studying their differences. True, they all produced apples in season, but this one was taller than that one. This one's branches curved together; that one's opened out. This one seemed to have a little face in the roughness of the bark; that one was smooth all the way. This one had a branch I could sit on easily; that one had such high branches I couldn't reach them. Each one had its own distinct identity and its own unique shape.

So it is with true spiritual and moral growth. When we become merely a mouthpiece for a group or leader, we may be expressing beautiful and profound ideas, but there is no freshness, no spontaneity, no hesitant groping from a born-within awareness. There is no true awakening and therefore no real growth.

There is no short-cut for the awakening process. I am convinced that most of the wrong, even cruel, things we do, arise not from deliberate destructiveness or delight in evil, but from parts of our selves which are literally not awake. I am struck by the fact that confessed and convicted murderers usually do not show, or apparently feel, any special deep agony, wrath, or revenge motivating their murders. They come across in interviews as bland, apparently feeling little or nothing. Their victims are not quite real to them. Other

NEW MORAL DISCOVERY

people are just objects out there. They seem to wonder what all the fuss is about.

Many of those who owned and dealt with slaves said, and perhaps quite genuinely believed, that the slave was not quite human and did not feel things as "we" do. When a slave child was sold away from its mother, neither, it was argued, would suffer as much as "civilized" people suffer. (I ponder this complacent, comfortable thinking, when I see calves and lambs taken from their mothers to be slaughtered.)

Those who cheat others, exploit others, sexually abuse others seldom think of the other person as being *real*. The ability to feel and identify with the actual reality of the other is unawakened, still in embryonic form.

I remember distinctly, as a tiny child, catching a fly and tearing off its wings. I did not do this in anger. I did not do it in order to inflict pain. It really didn't occur to me that it *was* painful for the fly. It was plain curiosity. I wanted to see what this flying object out there would do if it couldn't fly anymore. It wasn't real to me as a living being. It was only an object—a legitimate target for my curiosity.

I was reminded of this when I saw on television not long ago a program on birds and the reasons for their singing. The first half of the program was fascinating, as it showed scientists with tape recorder and camera watching and observing birds in their natural surroundings. My feelings underwent an abrupt change

ON THE ROAD TO SPIRITUAL WHOLENESS

when I watched them bring living birds into the laboratories, remove their vocal cords so they could not sing, shut them up in dark cages without any light for long periods, or isolate them from other birds for life. All this was done to observe if and how the vocal patterns and behavior would change. A horror grew in me. It was as if an inner light clicked on as a deeper consciousness grew. Something was *shown* to me—and out of that inner showing, the moral question was asked: Do we have the right to kill, mutilate, isolate, assault any living creature out of mere curiosity?

I am not talking now about experiments and development of vaccine for diseases. I am not talking about eating meat if and when we need it. I am talking about an awakening *spirit* of unity with every living thing—a feeling of compassion and a feeling of reverence. I am talking about the spirit which inwardly blesses and thanks the living creature whose life we may have to take to give nourishment or to prevent disease. *As this new moral shape begins to take place within us, we look at and touch each human being, each animal, each plant in a different way!*

Many of us who do not do violent acts nevertheless also often live lives of almost complete unawareness. We may think and speak in categories, tight compartments: "You know what men are . . . " or "Women always . . ." or "Just a teen-ager . . ." or "Little old ladies . . ." or "Black people always act as if . . ." or "Whites never can . . .". People who speak this way

NEW MORAL DISCOVERY

are unawakened people, mouthing phrases, pasting on labels. They are like sleepwalkers unaware of the infinite variations, the vitality, the unexpectedness of the world around them.

There are exceptions, of course. There are some people who *are* aware of the pain they inflict, and feel deep satisfaction at the pain. In these people, it is not that the awareness of the reality of other is unawakened or in embryonic form, but rather that the awakened sensitivity is deeply perverted, twisted out of shape, distorted almost beyond recognition. This usually comes from unfaced, unhealed anger and fear, which perhaps came at an age too young for the person to understand or bear it. The joy in the pain of others came as a cancerous growth on the tissue of defensiveness. If such a cancer grows in our spirit, so that the very God-given energy in us becomes an abuse to others, then it is as Jesus said: "If your eye is not sound, your whole body will be full of darkness. If then the light in you is darkness, how great is the darkness!" (Matt. 6:23) In such a case, we need more than awakening. We need to face it, to know that God loves us even so and can heal us, and then ask for divine radical surgery from his hands.

But for most of us, most of the time, it is merely sleep and insensitivity from which we are awakened. We are shown a clear picture of what is happening. Sometimes it comes with a shock of pain: "How could I have been so blind? Why didn't I realize?" A woman who had just

ON THE ROAD TO SPIRITUAL WHOLENESS

scraped out several platefuls of leftovers into the garbage suddenly remembered a photograph of a starving child in Biafra. A deeper level in her came awake. A light clicked on. A question was asked simultaneously: Is this the will of God? There was sudden clarity. There was also sudden agony. In great pain she put down the dishes, went and sat down with her family, and shared what she was seeing. They decided as a family to eat a little less and to use the extra money to support a child in need.

Sometimes the inner picture, the moral awareness, comes with inner joy, a sense of things falling into place. The inner knowledge that it is time to say yes to another person, or yes to a challenge or to a commitment, usually comes with deep, awakened joy *if* that person or that commitment is right for us. With joy, rather than pain, we say with the blind man healed by Jesus: "One thing I know, that though I was blind, now I see" (John 9:25).

Sometimes the inner moral awakening comes with no special pain or joy, but with slow assurance as we observe developing facts and realities after prayer. Such a moral assurance came to me as I prayed and pondered about the question of sexual decision. It was not a question about my own life. Long ago I had been shown what was right for *me*. But I was puzzled in my counseling of young people—fine, conscientious young people—who genuinely believed we had grown past the old laws against sexual sharing before marriage. To

NEW MORAL DISCOVERY

many of these young people, earnest in their desire to grow spiritually, the sexual sharing was just one other way of sharing love and fellowship. Even church leaders seemed divided on that question: What is the answer of Christ's spirit for *these* days?

I grew into an answer quietly and firmly one day as I sat talking with a young woman about prayer. A clear picture rose from the deep places as I talked.

"Prayer is a channel of communication with God," I found myself saying. "If there is a shallow communication, that means there is a block somewhere. You have confided to me that you have moved from one sexual relationship to another several times in recent years. The sexual relationship of man and woman is one of the *symbols* of the soul's relationship with God. This is made quite clear in both the Old and New Testaments. If we are without commitment in the sexual relationship, might that symbolize that we are without deep commitment to God? Could that be *your* block?"

A moral shape had taken place within me, as I saw the clear picture that sexual exchange is an exchange of the profoundest kind of energy of body and spirit. That kind of exchange made in a context without commitment perverts energies which were meant to be of vast significance into shallow meaninglessness.

But what if we grow into a moral awareness, but cannot yet act on it? This is a problem, an agony for many. They see a clear picture, they feel the moral shape taking place within, yet cannot express it in action.

"I released some things to God last week," a man once told me. "Now I realize I wasn't being honest with myself or with God. I'm not ready to give up those things yet. I can't."

As he talked, I was remembering that wonderful old story, dating back a couple of centuries, in which the young Quaker came to the old Quaker for spiritual counsel. "I love to go to the Friends' Meeting," the young man said. "I open myself to the Inner Light. But one thing I cannot bring myself to do. I can't yet cast aside my sword. I don't plan to kill anyone with it, but my father gave it to me, and his father before him. I can't give it up."

The old Quaker listened patiently and sat in silent prayer for a few minutes. Then he answered quietly: "Wear the sword. *Wear it as long as thee can!*"

This is profound spiritual and moral counsel. He knew that if the young man regularly and sincerely opened his heart and spirit to the Inner Light, he would so change and grow that the day would come when it would no longer seem desirable or natural to put on that sword. The need to cling to that symbol of force and bloodshed would drop off as a scab drops off a healed wound.

I thought over my own life, how often an inner struggle had gently and completely resolved itself as I grew. How often, as God's Spirit expands within us, we out-

NEW MORAL DISCOVERY

grow something that had seemed so powerful and irresistible. We look back on these early struggles as we look back on our fights in kindergarten or our early anxieties. We wonder why we were so worried. Just as moral growth is not a mere matter of outer obedience, neither is it a mere matter of will power. Just as nature enlarges and matures our bodies, *so Christ, the divine yeast, is working on us and enlarging us from within, if we pray for him to do so!*

We should not do violence to ourselves to force moral growth. We may have to force ourselves from harming or assaulting *others*, as Jesus made very clear. But to prevent ourselves from harming others is definitely not the same as forcing growth and insight in ourselves. Many people confuse these two things, and it is a serious mistake.

Remember the parable of Jesus (Matt. 13:24-30) about the servant who reported to the landowner that new weeds were growing up among the new wheat. Shouldn't he go out and tear up the weeds? The landowner said no. At this point of growth, to tear out the weeds would be to tear out a lot of the wheat as well. They would have to wait till a later stage of growth, and then the landowner himself would decide how to divide them. Jesus was pointing out that in many cases much must be healed, much must mature before we are ready to be parted from something that had been precious to us in the days of our fragmentation.

We must not assault ourselves. We must not try to

ON THE ROAD TO SPIRITUAL WHOLENESS

"slay the ego" ourselves. Trust the Lord of the inner harvest to separate the weeds from the wheat in us. In our early days of growing, often we literally cannot tell whether something is a weed or wheat. For example, many spiritually growing people are quick to judge themselves as "selfish" and try to kill such impulses within themselves, not realizing that they may be experiencing a God-given gift to love and care for the self in a new way.

We can tell God of our uncertainty, offer him what we honestly can, and each day open again the subconscious self for healing. We can ask that the "weeds" in us (whatever is wrong for us) be removed by his loving power growing within us, and that it become increasingly unnecessary to us. And we can ask that whatever is right for us be made increasingly clear and strong.

And if we do pray that way, he will take us at our word! Many are the surprises that lie ahead! The changes that take place within us will be joyous, painful, amusing, increasingly natural, and—above all—inwardly authentic.

But will the specific answers into which we grow be the same for *all* growing people? It would certainly be naïve to say that all spiritually mature people agree on all issues. Deep are the divisions on many basic issues and their solutions. Does that mean that God is saying one thing to me and another thing to you? Among those concerned about world hunger, is the man who refuses meat more mature spiritually than the man who eats it?

NEW MORAL DISCOVERY

Or is God speaking to them differently? Or what if two women in a prayer group differ deeply on abortion? One feels it is murder to kill the unborn baby, and the other feels that there are cases in which abortion is morally justifiable. Does that mean that one is necessarily spiritually superior to the other one, or that God has spoken to them differently?

We need not draw such conclusions. Our moral response to an inner picture shown us will grow and deepen as we grow and deepen. Where we are today, the way we respond today under Christ's guidance, is in a greater, wider place than it was yesterday. Tomorrow new levels of response may open to us, and we will be in a wider place yet. We cannot judge what place a neighbor is in, or from where he has come. His specific response to a moral question may be a different from *your* response, but it may represent a great awakening and deepening for *him*.

I know a man for whom it was a moral awakening of a sort to learn to appreciate the art of wine making. He learned, through that medium, to savor an experience slowly and thoughtfully. He became aware of the blending of the senses in a new way which was helpful to his hurried, breathless spirit. But now he is growing past that, out of that. As his deep spirit expands, it is more helpful, more natural to him now to say no rather than yes to that wine. But the basic learning experience, the slow savoring of the moment, has stayed with him in other ways.

ON THE ROAD TO SPIRITUAL WHOLENESS

Does that mean he is more spiritually atune to God's voice now than before? No, it means that all along he has been willing to learn, to change, to grow. *And that willingness is the basic moral response to life.*

It is not through this or that specific act or decision by itself that we primarily judge whether we are growing morally. Rather the question is, is there a new spirit expanding in us? A spirit that increasingly reveres life in all its forms? A spirit that breaks down walls that divide us inwardly and separates us from others? A spirit that not only accepts but embraces life? A spirit of deepening joy, sensitivity, compassion? A spirit ready to learn and change? It is out of this spirit of love and compassion that specific decisions can be eventually worked out in a spiritually growing community.

If we observe a spirit of bitterness, hostility, and exclusiveness growing in or among us, then we can be very sure that no matter how "spiritual" and exalted our opinions may be, it is not the *Christ* spirit in us, and our moral "growth" is not true growth at all.

It is the *direction* in which we are going that matters. It is the *direction* we take that indicates to us whether we are morally growing or not. Here are some test questions we can ask ourselves or our community about the basic direction of our decisions and actions if we are unsure about our path.

First, is this chosen action repressing other parts of me? Is it limiting my free choice, my power to love deeply, my power to communicate deeply?

NEW MORAL DISCOVERY

Second, is this decision or action of mine manipulating others, or limiting the free choice of others, or treating others like objects?

Third, is this action preventing me from fulfilling my ordinary responsibilities?

Fourth, is it hurting my physical health or that of others?

Fifth, is it leading me increasingly to a life without commitment?

Sixth, is it making it necessary for me to lie and deceive?

Seventh, is it coming from my deepest center as far as I can discern it, or from a fragmented part of me?

Eighth, is it closing my door to new growth, new change, new answers?

If we have to say yes to any of these test questions, then we can be quite sure that the direction we are going is not that of creative moral growth, but that our spirit is being deeply assaulted.

It is time to turn directly to the hands of Christ the Physician, and ask that our divisive, assaulting, repressive, distorting energies be healed and renewed by the limitless outpouring of his own energy and light.

> Into the hands which broke and quickened the bread, which blessed and caressed little children, which were pierced with the nails; into the hands which are like our hands . . . but which we know will always obey and reveal impulses filled with kindness and will always clasp us ever more closely . . . ; into the gentle and mighty

ON THE ROAD TO SPIRITUAL WHOLENESS

hands which can reach down into the very depth of the soul, the hands which fashion, which create, the hands through which flows out so great a love: into these hands it is comforting to surrender oneself, especially if one is suffering or afraid. And there is both great happiness and great merit in so doing.[1]

---

[1] Pierre Teilhard de Chardin, *Hymn of the Universe* (New York: Harper & Row, 1961), pp. 133-34.

Chapter 5
Test Signs of Spiritual Growth

There are defninite signs when we start growing into new spiritual wholeness. They are as definite as signs of new bodily health. And it is well for us to take occasional inventory of these various developing signs.

Nevertheless, this is a dangerous chapter for readers, because they may have a tendency to scan the list anxiously, checking off each point like an item on a grocery list, thinking, "Oh dear, I don't have that development yet! Something must be terribly wrong! Maybe I'm not growing at all!"

Such lists, like weight and height charts, can be misleading. There is really no such creature as an aver-

ON THE ROAD TO SPIRITUAL WHOLENESS

age person. We are all unique and individual. Our growing is organic, alive. It is bound to be lopsided and uneven. When I was worrying once about my own lopsidedness, and wondering why one part of me seemed so mature and another part so completely infantile, a wise minister reminded me that a lemon bush produces simultaneously the blossom, the green fruit, and the full-grown ripe lemon. One bush contains at the same time all the varying stages of development!

So let us reassure and comfort ourselves at the very beginning of our inventory, and remember that in some of these spiritual fruits we may be highly developed, and in others we may be only at the bare beginning. And that is as it should be. As I explained earlier in the book, we are as the First Psalm describes us—a tree growing by the water, producing fruit *in its season*. We cannot rush our seasons or our fruits. In God's own time (and he has all the time there is) all fruits and gifts will grow. The reason for such a list is to make clearer to ourselves in what general *direction* we are going and growing. Even if we see a change in only one of these categories, it is a sign that growth is taking place.

Let's look first at our *physical selves*. Are we becoming more aware that the body is meant to be a "temple" of divine energy? Do we know now that each organ, each cell is meant to contain and radiate the light of God? Do we begin to feel that the body is not an enemy or a puzzling stranger or our tyrannical master, but rather a beautiful, vibrant organism, blessed by God,

TEST SIGNS OF SPIRITUAL GROWTH

and given to us for a few years so that our spirit may be manifest through it in this material universe?

Do we begin to believe deeply that God has never wished us to be ill or in pain? Do we realize yet that through Jesus' actions we see that God longs, far more than we, that all shall be healed? Do we know now that healing can actually take place as we learn increasingly to say yes on all our levels of being?

Are we learning some methods of deep relaxation, so that the muscles do not strive against one another? Are we giving more attention to the healthfulness of our eating and drinking? Are some harmful physical habits beginning to lose their grip and drop away? Are some health problems beginning to clear up? When we do need a doctor's care occasionally, are we able to accept it with gratitude and the kind of humility that is willing to receive from another person?

Are our five senses becoming more alive and alert and aware? Do colors begin to seem brighter and clearer? Do we enjoy more our touching, tasting, smelling, hearing? Does the material world around us seem more clear, more fascinating, more precious? And yet, at the same time, are we less dependent on these things, less fussy and greedy?

Even as the body becomes more precious and beautiful to us, are we able at the same time to become less concerned about it? Or are we still apt to worry about disease and to become obsessed with the latest health diets and medicines? Are we learning to "listen" to the

ON THE ROAD TO SPIRITUAL WHOLENESS

body, and understand the signals it gives us that we are overworking, overresting, overeating or undereating, or experiencing too much stress? Are we beginning to be able to "release" the body to God's light and energy several times during the day? Does our sleep become more refreshing? Do we begin to become "friends" with our own physical type and accept it, or do we still compare our bodies with others and wish that we were different?

Let's turn to the *emotional self*. Are we increasingly aware of our real feelings of anger, pain, fear, worry, loneliness, guilt, reluctance, dislike, desire, joy, pleasure, comfort? Can we face and accept whatever feelings we have? Have we learned to look on our feelings as our inner children, not as demons or tempters?

Are we learning to take the responsibility for these inner feelings and not blame other people for them? Are we learning to bring these feelings into God's light with honesty and compassion, and release them into his light for healing?

Are we willing to have limitations and tired times without guilt? Are we able to accept the quiescent times, the fallow times when nothing much seems to be happening, without acute anxiety?

Are we able to accept the pain of growth and increasing sensitivity without being shattered or depressed? Are we learning what to do with painful memories that begin to surface? Or do we get trapped by the same old syndrome of anger and fear and guilt?

TEST SIGNS OF SPIRITUAL GROWTH

Have we learned the difference between a sin and an inner block or sickness? When we confess a sin, a destructive act done when we knew we were free to do otherwise, we feel a strong relief and release (though painful) when we confess it to God, the self, and maybe one other person. It is like the lancing of an abscess—there is healing in the pain. But when we confess a sickness or block, the dull, heavy ache continues. Then we know we need God's healing rather than forgiveness.

Do we feel growing conviction that God really loves us at this present moment, no matter in what state of unloveliness we may be? That he knows all about us and still loves us forever? Do we feel a growing confidence in God's work in our selves, and refuse to let others push us or assume authority over us?

What's happening with our *relationships?* Are we becoming aware that there are really other living people out there, and that they are hurting and enjoying just as much as we are? Do we feel a growing desire to reach out to these others and to be reached?

Are separating walls beginning to go down? Are we able to listen to what another person is saying? Are we beginning to be in touch with what others are feeling?

Are we willing to allow them to feel what they feel and be where they are? Do we begin to feel a growing reluctance to push or manipulate others "for their own good" or for our own ends?

Are we aware that we can't even inwardly categorize

others, decide about them, judge them, or prescribe for them? Are we able to release them from our own preconceptions and pictures? Are we really willing to leave them in God's hands?

Paradoxically, are we willing to open doors to them and share alternative ways with them to help them to their own unique wholeness? Mahatma Gandhi once said: "Our prayer for others ought never be 'God give them the light thou hast given to me', but rather 'Give them all the light they need for their own highest development.' "

Are we willing to receive help from others when we need it? Are we willing to show our weaknesses and share our feelings without guilt and shame? Can we learn from others?

Can we feel relaxed in the company of those who do not believe all that we believe, or who disagree with us on basic issues? Can we talk about it with openness and calm, knowing that only God has the ultimate answers? Can we increasingly look others straight in the eye as equals, and not try to make them into parents or spiritual authorities, no matter how good and wise they are?

What about *activities and decisions?* Are we willing to accept the probability of change, even if it hasn't happened yet? Are new energies, new interests, new possibilities beginning to open up?

Are we willing to have new doors open and some old doors close? What doors have actually opened this past year? What actual doors have closed? It is as important

TEST SIGNS OF SPIRITUAL GROWTH

to know what we are growing *out* of as to know what we are growing *into*.

Are we willing and eager to make plans without being compulsive and possessive about those plans? Are we willing to allow some ambiguity and mystery in our future? Are we becoming more open-ended about the future, and even willing to be surprised?

Is our rest period after work a time of grateful peace and refreshment, or is it guilty and restless? Is our work increasingly creative and fulfilling and *natural* to us? If not, that may be a sign that we have made a mistake in our commitment.

Do we accept and revere our freedom of decision and will as God's greatest gift to us, and refuse to allow it to be tampered with?

What about *moral growth?* This was dealt with thoroughly in the preceding chapter. Perhaps the moral growth question could be summed up by asking ourselves: Am I growingly aware of my oneness with the world, other people, animals, plants, soil, water, atmosphere, and my responsibility to be in creative harmony with them? Do I feel a growing reverence and tenderness for all living things? *What actions and decisions have actually changed this past year as a result?*

Is our *prayer life* becoming more natural and relaxed, less strained and pressured? Is it becoming a genuinely central source of energy and refreshment?

Are we willing to be our own honest self in prayer,

ON THE ROAD TO SPIRITUAL WHOLENESS

showing the true feelings and needs? Are we able to be silent and to listen?

Are we aware that God is doing most of the work in prayer in us and through us, and that *results are not all up to our own will power or positive feelings?* Do we increasingly believe that by the act of prayer divine energy is entering us, changing us, and thus the world around us?

What about our *commitments?* Are we becoming aware of the difference between the fragmented selves and the deep self? Do we delay a commitment until we are sure it has the consent of our *whole* self, refusing to be pushed into commitment out of guilt, perfectionism, or pressure from others?

Are we becoming aware that some of the deepest energies, such as sexuality, are to be expressed only in a committed relationship?

Are we willing to admit it and change if we have made a mistake in the life-style through which we chose to express our commitment?

Are we aware that commitment to God does not necessarily mean a specially prescribed line of action, such as the ministry or missions or social work? God will reveal to us many alternatives.

Are we able to be honest with God about what we can and cannot, at this moment, really commit to him?

Is our *awareness expanding?* Are we willing to let God show us new, unexpected frontiers of his work in creation? Are our horizons being pushed back in our

TEST SIGNS OF SPIRITUAL GROWTH

thinking about the seen and unseen aspects of the universe? What definite new insights have come to us about God, the self, the purpose of our life, guidance, prayer, death, experience after death, unseen forces of good and evil?

This kind of growing might come under the category of *wisdom*, which is not to be confused with degrees of education or intellectuality. Wisdom, basically, is openness to the harmony of God's divine law only partly manifested through physical laws, moral laws, psychological laws, psychic laws. As I observe this strange universe, it seems to me that God has given us free will not only to develop good-will, but also to learn how all these various laws of life fit together at a deep level in divine harmony, and to learn how to cooperate with this divine order.

It is striking that many of the criteria given here for the testing of spiritual growth are the same as those given in any test of emotional and psychological health. But this is as it should be. God is not *merely* interested in visions, psychic and mystical experiences, speaking in tongues, prophetic utterances, ability to preach and pray eloquently, pious and loving feelings, enthusiastic church attendance, benevolent gifts of money, observing the Ten Commandments, though often we speak of him as if these things compassed the range of God's concern. These things may or may not signify spiritual growth. *God is interested in our wholeness as human beings.* He is interested in whether our love for ourselves and others is *love come of age.* He is interested in whether we are receiving the gift of his divine energy and allowing it to heal our inner fragmentation and distortions. We cannot progress into the next step of spiritual evolution that God has planned for us until our human self is accepted, loved, healed in all its parts.

The basic question which sums up all these other questions might be: *In recent months, what special things have I allowed God's healing hands to do for me and through me?*

Remember—above all—that spiritual growing is not a matter of strain and tension. If there is chronic tension present, we can be fairly sure that the energy at work within us is not God's energy but rather the energy produced by anxiety, guilt, or group pressure.

A wise little book written in the last century, *The Christian's Secret of a Happy Life* by Hannah Smith, lays deep stress on this point.

> Imagine a child possessed of the monomania that he would not grow unless he made some personal effort after it, and who should insist upon a combination of ropes and pulleys whereby to stretch himself up to the desired height. . . . Growing is not a thing of effort, but is the result of an inward life principle of growth. All the stretching and pulling in the world could not make a dead oak grow. But a live oak grows without stretching. It is plain, therefore, that the essential thing is to get with-

TEST SIGNS OF SPIRITUAL GROWTH

in you the growing life, and then you cannot help but grow. And this life is the life hid with Christ in God, the wonderful divine life of an indwelling Holy Ghost. Be filled with this . . . and, whether you are conscious of it or not, you must grow, you cannot help growing. . . . Abide in the Vine. Let the life from Him flow through all your spiritual veins. Interpose no barrier to His mighty life-giving power, working in you all the good pleasure of His will.[1]

Some people find it helpful to go over these testing questions with a trusted friend in order to get an objective opinion, some feedback, in the spiritual check-up. This is a fine idea *if* it is understood that the friend is in no way a spiritual authority or director. He is only to give you with honesty and openness his own observations about you, and whether he is aware of any change in you in these areas. It is hard to be always clear-sighted and honest with ourselves, and sometimes we think we have made great progress in some areas, and find to our astonishment it is not getting across to others at all. Or, we may feel we have come to a standstill in something, and don't realize how much we actually have changed in the eyes of others. Obviously the friend we ask to do the check-up with us should be someone who has known us over a fairly long period of time and who is himself or herself a well-balanced person with some awareness of spiritual growth.

[1] Hannah Whitall Smith, *The Christian's Secret of a Happy Life* (New York: Grosset and Dunlap, 1884), pp. 152, 156-57.

ON THE ROAD TO SPIRITUAL WHOLENESS

What if we find that rapid changes are occurring on many fronts in ourselves? Are we in danger of pride? Are we riding for a fall? Many people are genuinely suspicious and worried about signs of strong positive growth. This fear is related to an age-old superstition that the heavenly powers are jealous of earthly joys, powers, beauty, and fruitfulness, and if we become too aware of these things in our lives, they will probably be taken away.

This is the old ingrained distrust and fear of God that blocks so much of what he is trying to do for us. God is the *source* of all true joys, powers, beauty, and fruitfulness. He rejoices in their manifestation in our lives far more than we do. He will no more condemn or punish us for our gladness than we would punish our baby for the bursting, beaming pride he shows as he takes his first staggering steps alone!

The kind of pride and joy we feel in genuine growth is not the kind of pride that separates us from other people or causes us to put them down. That is a destructive, *un*joyful thing, and we learn quickly as we grow how to discern its symptoms. No, this is the kind of objective joy and thankfulness we feel at seeing *any* beautiful thing coming into fruitfulness and fulfillment. If we can look at a flowering fruit tree and feel delighted thankfulness, we can also look at a beautiful new growth of love, courage, and peacefulness within ourselves with equal delight. It is all God's doing any-

TEST SIGNS OF SPIRITUAL GROWTH

way, so what does it matter whether it takes place outside ourselves or inside ourselves? We need not become all falsely modest or glumly cautious simply because the miracle of God's growth can be seen in our bodies and in our hearts and minds.

Chapter 6
The Free Christian and Group Commitment

If spiritual and moral growth is such a personal and unique act of God's Spirit in a human being, what place is there for groups? Are they irrelevant for our deep growing? Or, worse, do they actually threaten the freedom and uniqueness of our growing?

Any great gift of God carries with it a potential danger. The greater the gift, the more grave the danger, as pointed out in the first chapter. It is naïve and sentimental to suppose otherwise. The possible abuse and danger is a necessary part of our essential freedom of choice. It appalls me sometimes to realize the risks God is willing to take by giving us freedom. Take the power of parenthood, for example. The su-

THE FREE CHRISTIAN AND GROUP COMMITMENT

preme power over the child's body and emotions is in the hands of the parent in the early years. All that the growing consciousness of the helpless child will receive of love, security, good-will—or their opposites—will come through the channeling of the parent. What he feels about other people, the world around him, God, is first molded by the acts and attitudes of that human being, the parent. What hair-raising freedom and power is given to the parent! What stupendous risks God is taking! But if we are to be free, if we are to learn and grow in creative power in any *real* way, such risks must be taken.

It is the same with the very real power of groups. When the emotional, psychic, and spiritual energy fields of separate individuals merge with one another in any group situation, the power experienced and released is far stronger than the individual can experience alone. And of course, that power can be used for either good or evil, for creation or compulsion.

We have experienced this blending and merging of our separate energy fields in exciting sports events, when the spectators feel swept out of their separateness and bound together in the thrill and enthusiasm. It can be felt in a theater where we are watching great drama, a rising above our separate identity and blending in the emotional power the actors are projecting. Many great actors have reported feeling this power, greater than themselves, binding them and the audience temporarily into one body. We have heard reports

ON THE ROAD TO SPIRITUAL WHOLENESS

of the real power of a mob spirit when a group is bound together in a destructive hatred far beyond what each would feel individually. Politicians, and ministers too, can almost palpably feel the moment when their listeners are bound together into a unity which receives and feeds back, as if from one soul and personality. Cynical leaders know well how to develop and manipulate this power which results from group merging.

If this power is experienced in sports, drama, and politics, how much more powerfully it can be experienced in a group committed to spiritual purposes, for in such groups the deepest energies of the universe are received and channeled. But God gives us the freedom to use it as we will, always. How incredible the creative good it can offer! How devastating the evil of which it is capable? Atomic power is nothing in comparison.

More, much more, should be written, preached, explained to us all how to use creatively the power potential of religious growth groups, and how to distinguish between the releasing group and the assaulting group. It should be explained to children, from the time they first begin to form their little neighborhood and school groups, how to tell if the experience is a healthy one for them. It should be explained to young people in their teens in their hunger for closeness to others. It should be explained to *all* people who begin to reach out and search in their spiritual hunger for groups to share in and affirm their search. *We all should be taught how to tell the releasers from the assaulters*—and we should

THE FREE CHRISTIAN AND GROUP COMMITMENT

be taught ahead of time, because once we are deeply *in* the energy field of a strong, spiritually assaulting group, it is almost impossible to observe clearly or to think independently. Whether this is because of brainwashing, I don't know.

I think what is happening is that we have merged ourselves deeply with the group spirit, or personality, and have chosen to let that personality possess and displace our own. We think the "thought" of the group. We speak with its voice. We see with its eyes and attitude. We call its commands the voice of God and we do not permit ourselves to hear any other voice which might disagree. It is like a case of possession, except that the possessor is not some disincarnate evil spirit, but the personality of the group we have chosen. It may not be evil at all in the obvious sense. In the examples given in the first chapter, those leaders were proclaiming pure and lofty doctrine, and their followers had given up many destructive personal habits. But they are evil in the sense that they always try to *possess* each follower as a part of the group life and spirit, forcing conformity and obedience, rather than using the group to *release* each member to his own unique response, timing, and fulfillment. And, of course, it is only when people are thus released to God's unique work with each of them that genuine growth takes place.

Nothing is more beautiful and helpful than such a releasing group. I realize how blessed I was in my very

ON THE ROAD TO SPIRITUAL WHOLENESS

first spiritual group, as a teen-ager. I had been an extremely shy, withdrawn child from birth. In my early teens I became slowly but intensely aware of the pervading love of God which healed me of many fears and awakened in me a real longing to grow closer to other people. That longing to reach out to others in a deep way is, sooner or later, *always* a part of spiritual growth. I joined a college church group, not out of any sense of guilt or duty, but in the awareness that I was ready to take this step. It seemed a natural and spontaneous thing to do.

And through that beautiful and nurturing group, for five years, God brought me into increasing wholeness as a human being. As I observe the assaulting groups proliferating so rapidly these days, I realize, as never before, my depth of gratitude to this very first group of faith in my life which so deeply channeled the freedom of God's love to me. From the very beginning I was shown in every possible way how a group can be profoundly dedicated and committed, and yet profoundly releasing to its members. Yes, it can be done!

What is the secret? I look back to this group in my early life, for an answer. *Neither the leaders nor any members assumed spiritual authority over any other member!* We had two leaders, yes. They (a husband and wife team) were strong, well trained, and gifted individuals. They walked closely with God, and were keenly aware of his presence through prayer, music, art, work, nature. They taught us how to seek and

THE FREE CHRISTIAN AND GROUP COMMITMENT

accept such closeness, how to relate to one another, and how to serve the world in its pain.

But *how* did they teach us these things? Never by long lectures. Never by command. Never by the power of their very real charm. Never by ridicule or rebuke. Actually they never did much actual talking or instructing. In group discussions they were usually quiet, listening with genuine interest to what was being said. I'm sure they were praying for all of us almost constantly, but that was not said overtly.

What *did* they do? They saw each one of us as beautiful, interesting, and unique, just where we were. They opened many doors of possible growth and experience, but never pushed us through those doors. They believed each one of us had something special to give in our growing, but it was up to us to discover what that special thing was. We were allowed to go forward or to draw back, and our times of quiescence were respected. Beautiful things of the spirit were offered, but no guilt trips were laid on us if we were not ready for the beautiful new things. With their background help, we planned our own programs and activities and elected our own officers, and we were allowed to learn from our mistakes. The only time we were limited in any way was if any of us tried to interfere with another's growth, or ever tried to exert pressure on another member. Many problems of faith and procedure were discussed openly, and everyone's opinion

ON THE ROAD TO SPIRITUAL WHOLENESS

was listened to and respected. We might disagree with one another, but we were still loved.

How free we were! And yet how committed—committed *to* that spirit of Christ which sets us free. Thirty years have gone by since then, and we who were members are still feeling the vitality and the power of that group which so deeply released us!

I compared my early experience to the tragic experience of a young woman who came to see me the other day. Her spiritual group, which she had served devotedly for several years, had just excommunicated her from their fellowship. Two of the leading members, who had been designated as "spiritual authorities" by the main leader, had called on her and accused her of spiritual pride. What was her crime? She had talked with a few other members who had come to her for some counseling help, instead of sending them at once to the proper "authorities." They claimed she was presumptuous and proud, and when she tried to explain and protest they told her her very feelings of protest were proof of her pride.

She tried to go to the main leader to talk things over, but he told her that any "appeal" had to come through the very leaders who were accusing her. Because she refused simply to confess and submit, she was ousted and all the other members were forbidden to speak to her, write to her, or even pray with her. They have all been told that the voice of the leaders (who are not even elected, but appointed) is the voice of God.

THE FREE CHRISTIAN AND GROUP COMMITMENT

This is by no means an unusual situation. I have heard similar stories three or four times in recent months. A young man from a different spiritual group told me that when he expressed doubts or disagreements with his group, he was advised to treat those doubts as temptations of Satan and give himself even more completely to the group for exorcism. Finally, he realized that his growing inner panic and sense of claustrophobia were probably signs of the crushing of his identity. He was still free enough to leave.

Groups like this are growing, in which doubts are designated as temptations, in which individual opinions and powers are condemned as pride, in which free personal decision is treated as rebellion. And this is happening in many of those same groups that have been showing indisputable power of prayer, power of healing, power of spiritual gifts of all kinds. All except the love which releases!

Is this surprising? Not really. It is an old story. Back in the earliest days of the Christian church, Paul wrote a letter to the believers in Corinth, warning them about this very problem. In chapters 12, 13, 14 of I Corinthians (which really ought to be read together as a whole) Paul warns them that it is quite possible to have all kinds of beautiful, powerful spiritual gifts and yet to be lacking love. Especially in chapter 13, he analyzes love, in its gentleness, its releasing power, its respect, as the most basic requirement for any kind of growing spiritual awareness.

ON THE ROAD TO SPIRITUAL WHOLENESS

So this chapter is really dealing with the most fundamental question of all about spiritual growth: *Are we ready to receive and give the love which releases?* We ask it of ourselves. We must also learn to use this question as the major testing point of any group we join.

Perhaps we can break this main question down into sub-questions to help us in our discernment.

First, in this group relationship do I feel really free? Or am I compelled or hurried along faster than I'm comfortable going?

Second, do I feel put down in this group? Do I feel as if I am being watched and judged?

Third, am I being flattered? Are others paying me more attention and praising me more than is realistic?

Fourth, does the world outside this group, other people, begin to seem unreal and far away? Am I taught to look on others outside the group as completely wrong or as targets for conversion?

Fifth, am I losing a sense of my separate identity? Am I beginning to feel that my needs, abilities, and feelings are unimportant?

Sixth, am I asked frequently to account for my actions? Do I feel sometimes as if I were being punished? (The philosopher Nietzsche once wisely said, "Beware of anyone in whom the desire to punish is predominant.")

Seventh, do I find myself beginning to decide for others, or domineer over them "for their own good"?

THE FREE CHRISTIAN AND GROUP COMMITMENT

If we must say yes to *any* of these questions, something is very wrong in our group relationship. We are in an unhealthy situation. The group may be teaching all manner of high moral and spiritual values. It may be loving and close knit. But the love it expresses is not the kind that releases, but rather the kind that makes us childish and dependent. It is the kind of love that says: "Give your life and freedom to us, and we will mold you into what you ought to be. Give yourself to us, and that will be the same as giving yourself to God, for God gives us spiritual authority over you!" This is spiritual assault!

Does this mean that there is no place for strong groups or strong leaders? Does this mean there is no place for firm convictions and vigorous witness and enthusiastic participation and loving closeness? By no means! Wherever genuine Christians rejoicing in the power of prayer get together, there will be love, power, enthusiasm. There is bound to be convinced and radiant witness. But such power is very different from the kind exerted by groups which consider themselves spiritual authorities.

Likewise, compare a marriage of radiant, vital love and closeness between two equal partners, and a marriage based on the bond of authority and submission. One can ask these same seven questions about one's marriage, one's friendships, the parent-child relationship, or *any* relationship, as well as about spiritual groups. One can ask these same questions about the

ON THE ROAD TO SPIRITUAL WHOLENESS

healthfulness of a psychic experience. We can ask them in a doctor-patient relationship or a business association. For the basic question being asked is: Are my freedom and identity being respected—and am I respecting the freedom and identity of others?

A vigorous, strong prayer leader is often tempted (as is a strong marriage partner or a business associate) to take over the lives and freedom of others. As a prayer leader for some years, I became quickly aware that there were many people who really wanted me to make their decisions for them. Many people would telephone or make appointments to see me, not merely to talk over their spiritual and personal problems, but to throw their whole selves into my hands. It was made very clear that I was to be emotionally, morally, and spiritually responsible for them. I was to be their source of strength and wisdom, and in return I was to get submission, imitation, flattery. This was not usually said in words, but there were ways in which it was made obvious that it was expected. It was then that I learned that the dominance of one person is not always the fault only of the domineering leader, but also of the submissive, almost masochistic, follower.

What can a spiritual group leader do when he is tempted in this way by some follower? He or she must do the same as a marriage partner must do, or a parent of grown children, or a friend or a doctor. He must offer love and concern. He must be honest and tell the truth about what he sees and feels, and offer alternatives of

THE FREE CHRISTIAN AND GROUP COMMITMENT

action. But he must refuse to become the host to a parasite. He must refuse to become responsible for any one else's emotional, moral, or spiritual decision.

If he feels a parasitic relationship has already developed, and the other person has ceased growing in freedom, he must share the problem with loving honesty and release himself. He must try to show the other person how to draw directly on the power of God within, and to release the other person from the fear of making mistakes. It is better to go one inch by our own decision than ten miles by someone else's will and power over us!

To be sure, there are emergency, temporary situations in which we do need to be carried by the strength of others, or to carry others. This can happen in times of great physical or emotional pain, times of radical withdrawal from destructive habits, times of crisis in relationships, when we give ourselves into the hands of others, or others give themselves to us, to be helped over the crisis with loving authority. I remember one time I was asked to help restrain a young woman going through the agony of withdrawing from alcohol. Another time, a woman facing divorce needed strong help as she fought with hysterics. A young man going through a psychotic panic needed our time, energy, and firm guidance for several days. But such crisis situations must be regarded as strictly temporary, as temporary as a physical need for crutches or for hospitalization for sudden illness. The leader or the group may

ON THE ROAD TO SPIRITUAL WHOLENESS

give the temporary "intensive care" with generosity and love, but also with an eye to the release and renewed independence of the person as soon as possible.

Occasionally there will be a person who, once having tasted the pleasures of being carried by a group, will not *want* to be released. He wishes to continue over a period of many weeks drawing on the time and energy of the group or leader. I have known of two or three groups destroyed because they allowed themselves increasingly to center around the personal problems of one member. They knew it to be their Christian responsibility to love and help one another, and thus they felt they must be willing to discuss the needs and concerns of that member and to help him as a group, without any limitation at all. Obviously this is as destructive as the opposite extreme of totally repressing or excluding that member. I feel we should deal with one another in our group as we try to deal with the "members" within ourselves—let each one be heard and respected, but allow no one to dominate, either with needs or opinions. If any member has a personal problem he or she wishes to share, let him *briefly* express it and feel the loving concern of all. But instead of endlessly discussing, diagnosing, and prescribing, let the group turn soon to the problems of others as well—and then let *all* problems be brought in prayer to the Source of light and healing. Encourage one another to look *within* for the growing answers to be revealed, rather than depending on advice from others.

THE FREE CHRISTIAN AND GROUP COMMITMENT

The counsel of the great mystic Joel Goldsmith concerning spiritual leadership has always been of tremendous help to me in my relationship with others:

> Always remember, it matters not one whit what your past experience may have been. It is not sufficient to warrant you in advising anybody about his personal affairs. Say "Now let us meditate and bring the Christ to bear on the situation.". . .
> Bring to bear your divine sonship, and out of the hidden manna those who come to you for help will be directed, led, protected, sustained.
> Have you the right to tell another person that he must live by the standards that you have achieved through years of struggle, strife, seeking, searching? No. Give him of your hidden manna and let the Christ appear to him in the form necessary for his unfoldment. . . .
> The offering of the wine, the water, and the meat must be done gently, sparingly, permitting the other person to come in his own good time to his spiritual good.[1]

If this is the foundation upon which a spiritual group is built, we will be true channels to one another of God's releasing love.

---

[1] Joel Goldsmith, *Leave Your Nets* (New York: Julian Press, 1964).

Chapter 7

A Suggested Spiritual Retreat or Workshop

When a strongly motivated group gathers together for a spiritual retreat or workshop, great energies will be released, breakthroughs will be experienced, lives will be changed. "Retreat" is really the wrong word for what is happening. It is an *advance* on the profoundest level. It is intensive advance into awareness of the self, its energies and its needs. It is an advance into awareness of God—his compassion, his healing radiance, his challenge.

There are many different ways and methods, of course, by which group members can share and channel these energies to one another. Some are large groups;

A SUGGESTED SPIRITUAL RETREAT

some are very small. Some are ecumenical; some are of only one denomination. Some are open to all ages and both sexes; some are limited to only one sex or one age group. Some make room for physical activity and manual creativity together; some have only the exchange of thought and words. Some emphasize silence; others encourage much verbal sharing. Some have strong, experienced leaders in charge; others share leadership among the members.

There is a need and a place for all these different kinds of spiritual gatherings. But it is my opinion that certain basic understandings are necessary if the intensive experience shared is to be one of true spiritual growth rather than one of spiritual pressure and assault.

1. Though there may be a leader, no one in the group is to have spiritual authority over anyone else. Nor does the group itself have spiritual authority over any member.

2. Each person present is to be respected at the point where he or she is. No specific response, experience, or emotion is to be "programmed" or demanded.

3. Though honest sharing is to be encouraged, no one is to be pushed into speaking or sharing.

4. When feelings and experiences are shared, no one is to be judged, diagnosed, or prescribed for. The person sharing is to be listened to and accepted lovingly.

5. No one person may dominate the whole time and energy of others with his problems and ideas. After a

reasonable time of sharing, the person sharing may be gently reminded that there are others to be heard from.

6. There should be some time allowed for group silence and individual privacy. This may be anywhere from a half hour to several hours depending on the length of the time together.

7. Even if silence is emphasized, there should be some time provided in which members may talk together or talk things over with the leaders.

8. Though the time should be well organized, it should not be so rigidly structured that there is no room for unexpected experiences, sharings, or developments which the group may wish to explore.

9. The intensity and depth should not be stiff and solemn. Where growth is experienced, there is considerable laughter, joy, amusement, and occasional spontaneous tears. In long retreats there should be time provided for real relaxation: games, reading, walking, music, art projects, and sleep.

10. Though the leader will share insights and give guiding suggestions, *the keynote for everyone is learning to listen to one another, to the selves within, and to the inner Christ.*

These ten foundation points are, I feel, necessary for the spiritual health of *any* retreat or workshop. When any of these points are neglected or abused, there enters spiritual abuse or assault.

The suggested outline for retreats that now follows, however, *is not to be taken as a rule for all retreats*. It

A SUGGESTED SPIRITUAL RETREAT

is put forward as one among many helpful procedures. It can be adapted to the two or three hours of a workshop, or the two or three days of the average retreat. It can be expanded, contracted, or modified to fit the age group or the type of background and experience of the members attending. It is a way and method that I have found helpful and releasing, but it must be clearly understood that there are many alternative ways and methods. This approach is broken down into areas of major concern and awareness which the group may wish to think through, talk through, work through as they move toward spiritual wholeness.

Awareness of one another. It is well for each person to introduce himself briefly. If it is a small group, or if the members are already well known to one another, each might share briefly why he or she came to the retreat, with some mentioning of main concerns and expectations.

If the group is very large, or if the leader senses they are shy with one another at first, the members might write down (not to be handed in or read aloud) some of their feelings and expectations.

On one retreat I attended, where members were well known to one another, each drew a rough picture or symbol of how he felt at that moment and shared it. It was a delightful and healthfully honest way to begin. And it was most enlightening to see how many members felt a little tense and anxious about the retreat, or

ON THE ROAD TO SPIRITUAL WHOLENESS

still felt worried or exhausted from the day or week behind them.

Explanations and preparations. At this point, the leader or co-leaders can explain the meaning of a spiritual retreat or workshop as a meeting between the self and God. It can be explained that each person has been drawn there by God for a special reason, and each will experience something and be given something—though what is given will be different for each. Some will find their special gift and growth through the silence, some through the sharing, some through reading or writing or prayer. Some will have old memories healed. Some will be given new ideas or energies. Each person present is challenged to go deeper into the self and deeper into God.

The leaders can then explain the general procedure and schedule for the next few hours or days, and then invite questions and suggestions.

Awareness of God. Leaders may here suggest that members look closely at their true feelings about God, explaining that certain early associations, preconceptions, fears, or angers about God may be blocks to spiritual growth. This can be done in a non-reproving way by such discussion questions as: What were some of the thoughts about God that frightened us as children? What images come into our minds when we say 'God'? What kinds of feelings? If the group is reluctant to begin this honest sharing, the leaders can share some of their own early or existing hang-ups and associations

A SUGGESTED SPIRITUAL RETREAT

with the word "God". After a period of discussion, the leaders can read some of Jesus' parables and ask the group: "What was in the mind of Jesus, what did he mean by 'God'? What is he trying to get across to us?"

The hope is that at the very beginning of the retreat, the members will learn to be honest about what they really feel and will begin to realize that God's love is not something to be earned, but is already given without limit and without reservation.

Awareness of prayer. The leaders now in the same way can explore concepts of prayer and their attending hang-ups and problems. Members may be encouraged to share experiences of prayer, both good and bad.

Through scriptural passages, modern writings, or shared experiences, the leader may suggest (if it has not already come forth from the group) that prayer is not begging a reluctant God, but rather learning to open the self with honesty to God, so that he might heal us and give us what we need.

Small group sharing. At this point, it is helpful to break up into groups of three (if possible) to talk over the points and problems and suggestions raised and their own personal reactions, for perhaps a half hour. Then they may wish to come together into the larger group to share further insights and questions for another half hour.

Meditation and separation. If this is a workshop, the members may wish to break here for relaxation. If this

ON THE ROAD TO SPIRITUAL WHOLENESS

is the end of the first evening of a retreat, it is a good point at which to join in a closing meditation. The group can sit in a circle, with a lighted candle in their midst. The leader may suggest a few points on how to relax the body, how to put around the self the healing light of God, and with silence and peacefulness breathe in that light. The leader may call on the group for a few brief, spontaneous prayers, and then as the group stands with joined hands in a circle, the leader may dismiss them to a night of silence and peacefulness. They may then separate in silence.

If the retreat began in the morning, this period can close with a half hour of silence in which the members go off alone, and join together later for lunch.

Awareness and nurture of the feelings. When the group reassembles, there can be a short prayer together and a short period of sharing any special thoughts or problems that may have risen.

Now the leader can direct the attention to the hurting children within that God wishes to heal. The leader can ask each member to face silently or write down privately any special feelings, to listen to the feeling, and then bring it to the hands (or the light) of the healing Christ, as explained in chapter 3.

Awareness and healing of memories. The members now can be asked to select and face one or two unhealed memories, perhaps one from long ago and the other more recently.

A SUGGESTED SPIRITUAL RETREAT

It can be explained how God can reach out and touch that point of trauma or that hurt person within and heal him, for time does not exist to God. This should be done in a leisurely, slow-paced way. In my opinion it is better for the group to work on these inner aspects in silence at this time, except for the brief, guiding, reassuring suggestions of the leader.

Awareness and healing of the future. The members are asked to think of one or two events that will probably happen in the near future about which there may be some anxiety or uncertainty. In silence, the members are asked to release that future moment to God's hands and to visualize God's strength and guidance being there to meet them at that moment.

Releasing and healing of the subconscious. The leader can explain how God's love and awareness already embrace our subconscious selves, where the roots of so many problems lie. More light and healing can enter if we deliberately open the door and ask for it. The leader can encourage the members to do so, perhaps using the trap-door image suggested in chapter 3.

The members are asked to hold this or a similar image in mind, and to remember that not only are old wounds being healed, but new energies are being released by this act.

Break for discussion or separation. Depending on the type of group, the leader can now call for discussion

ON THE ROAD TO SPIRITUAL WHOLENESS

of the inner experience just shared, or dismiss the members for a period of privacy and meditation.

Break for relaxation or meal.

Listening to God. After a brief period of sharing and questions, the leader can draw the attention of the members to the problem of listening to God, now that they have learned how to listen to their inner selves.

The difference should be explained between the voice of emotion, the voice of duty, the voices of outside pressures and expectations, and the voice of God from within. Discussion can follow on experiences and opinions about these different voices and how to tell one from another.

The leader can suggest some of the characteristics of the ideas and guidance which come from God, such as: the sense of joy, the awareness of freedom and naturalness, the growing awareness of one's true self and other people, growing energy and meaningfulness, and growing and changing moral sensitivity, as discussed in chapter 4.

The group can be called on to think of further "tests" by which we can know if the guidance is truly from God.

Reassurance should be given to the group members that if nothing special occurs during meditation in the way of new ideas or inner guidance, they are not to worry or to push, but to relax and wait. Something will surface in the next few hours or days.

In some retreats at this point, I bring out slips of paper on which are typed a verse from the Bible, a line

A SUGGESTED SPIRITUAL RETREAT

from a hymn, or a quote from a book on prayer, and place them face down on the floor to be drawn at random by the members. These can be taken as special focal points for meditation. It is important that the quotations chosen express God's love and acceptance as well as his challenge.

Separation for meditation. The members may go off alone at this point for a time of deliberate opening of the self to listen to God. Perhaps a particular problem can be presented for guidance.

Members are not encouraged to read at this point (except their chosen quotation) but are challenged to sit or walk in silent relaxation and try to listen to the deepest levels within. They may wish to write down thoughts or symbolic images that come.

Long break for relaxation, eating, quiet talking, reading, sleeping, or exercise.

Channeling energy to others. After brief sharing, the group is now asked to turn the attention outward. It is time for the healing within to flow forth into the healing of others. The leader can ask the group to share experiences and problems of intercessory or "channeling" prayer. Attention should be drawn to the analogy between the process of healing within and healing for others through the following points:

1. Prayer for others, just like prayer for ourselves, is not begging God, but assuming that God already loves and wishes to heal us. His will to give is far greater than our will to receive.

ON THE ROAD TO SPIRITUAL WHOLENESS

2. It is important to pray for the *wholeness* of the other person, rather than just for specific symptoms to be healed. Outer symptoms usually arise from deep causes that we cannot see.

3. When we offer ourselves up as channels for God's healing light to be intensified in another's life, we should *release* that person into God's hands and not try to program a specific result.

4. If there is no immediate change or improvement, we must not accuse the other person or ourselves of lack of faith. Healing is not a simplistic matter, for there are many levels and energies to be healed before outer symptoms change, and it may take a long time.

5. Though we should be expectant of change, knowing that prayer releases true energy into life, the change may not always be what we have expected. The healing may be physical or it may be emotional or it may take place among relationships. Or it may be all these things. It may be sudden and complete in what the world calls a miracle, or it may be slow and partial because of blocks we cannot see or judge.

6. Anyone who prays for another should learn how to put himself under Christ's protecting energy and light (see Ephesians 6:10-18 and Psalm 91) so that he does not take the problem of the one for whom he is praying into his own body and emotions and thus exhaust his own energy.

7. Above all, remember that it is Christ who is the

A SUGGESTED SPIRITUAL RETREAT

healer. We are just the channels through which his healing radiance flows into the lives of others. A good way to begin a channeling prayer is to remember the words of Jesus in John 15:4, 5:

> Abide in me, and I in you. As the branch cannot bear fruit by itself, unless it abides in the vine, neither can you, unless you abide in me. I am the vine, you are the branches. He who abides in me and I in him, he it is that bears much fruit, for apart from me you can do nothing.

Channeling experience. Now the group can experiment with channeling prayer. They can sit in a circle with a chair in the middle, and the leader can say aloud, slowly, the name of each person present. During the short silence after each name, the whole group can focus and channel the thought of God's light on that person.

The leader can ask if anyone wants to sit briefly on the chair for the laying on of hands. (If the members are shy about beginning, the leader can sit on the chair to get them started.) Anyone who wishes can come forward to lay hands lightly on the head or shoulders of the person there, and offer up himself as a channel for about a minute or two. Usually several people come forward to lay on hands. The rest of the group, still seated, can hold up their hands toward the person in need, or mentally focus God's light on him. Usually after the first person has sat on the stool in the middle

ON THE ROAD TO SPIRITUAL WHOLENESS

many others will wish to do so. But if there is reluctance, the leader must be careful not to push or urge.

When everyone is seated again, the leader can ask the members to speak aloud names of people who are sick or in need of some sort. There should be a short silence after each name, as the group offers itself up as a channel for God's healing energy to intensify in that person's life.

Some may wish to mention political and national leaders. Others may mention disaster areas in the world. Others may mention special concerns close to their hearts. All this is good if done slowly, with relaxation and release, knowing that it is Christ who is at work.

The releasing farewell. In a retreat situation, it is deeply meaningful to conclude with a simple communion service in which two or three people share in the serving of the bread and wine. If this can't be done, light a candle and ask the group to join hands in a circle around it for final prayers, singing, and closing embraces or mutual blessings.

The energies of new life released in such a period of sharing are phenomenal. Often out of such an experience, an ongoing group can be formed which will meet regularly for sharing, prayer, silence, and channeling. But no one should be pushed into such a commitment. Some will wish to go their ways separately, but carrying in their hearts the divine yeast of a new life.

A SUGGESTED SPIRITUAL RETREAT

Churches which encourage annual or semiannual retreats or workshops of this kind will find in truth a new wine of joy, energy, release, and wholeness. They will discover together that the gift and voice and radiance of the Christ within is no dream, but a transforming reality.